REPORTING FROM THE
BRIDGE

REPORTING FROM THE
BRIDGE

Aydoğan Vatandaş

BLUE DOME

Published by Blue Dome Press
535 Fifth Avenue, Ste.601
New York, NY 10017-8019

www.bluedomepress.com

Library of Congress Cataloging-in-Publication Data
Vatandas, Aydogan, 1974-
  Reporting from the bridge / Aydogan Vatandas.
    p. cm.
  ISBN 978-1-935295-16-7 (pbk.)
  1. Journalism--United States--History--21st century. 2. Foreign news--United States. 3. Middle East--Press coverage--United States. 4. Journalists--United States--Interviews. 5. College teachers--United States--Interviews. I. Title.
  PN4867.2.V38 2012
  071'.3--dc23

                                                                            2012020117

ISBN: 978-1-935295-16-7

Printed by
Görsel Dizayn Ofset Matbaacılık Tic.Ltd.Şti., Istanbul - Turkey

CONTENTS

Foreword

Katharine Branning

It is hard to imagine that it has been only a few years since such words as Google, Kindle, IMS, app, Tumbler, blog, streaming, Flickr, Twitter, Facebook, and RSS have entered our vocabulary. It is even more surprising to see how in such a short time the concepts behind these formats of information exchange have altered the modern media platform. We now envision a future where libraries will be held on jump drives, where the call "roll the presses!" will no longer be heard in the land; where hand-held devices become pressrooms, and the print versions of newspapers and books will be looked upon by our children as museum relics when they visit the Smithsonian Institution on school trips.

The impact of social-based and user-generated sources of information on the current media landscape and their coexistence with the traditional print resources and journaled studies is a fascinating and complex issue facing the modern world. Yet it is certain that these two tendencies—the grounded approach of the established print news sources and the viral, hands-on reporting of events through the social media at large—must meet in a middle field. As each of these news venues offer a unique and valuable perception to the diffusion of information, the world of journalism must now scramble to best use of them to serve their audiences. Although the question of the continued hegemony of mainstream journalism is now a hot topic, the classical question of the demands of objective truth and the ethical onus of a journalist to tell it, remain the same. There lies the middle field.

A recent rereading of a medieval source brought the pertinence of this issue, at centuries distant, to a sharp focus. It is interesting to note that Ibn Khaldun, the famed late fourteenth century Islamic historian and philosopher, begins his magnum opus, the *Muqaddimah*, with a listing of seven of the difficulties that await the historian in his work. The same critical issues apply to journalists in their role as modern historians, and bear reviewing once more. Ibn Khaldun states that "All records, by their very nature, are liable to error, from partisanship towards a creed or opinion; over-confidence in one's sources; a failure to understand what is intended; a mistaken belief in the truth; the inability to place an event in its real context; the common desire to gain favor of those of high ranks, by praising and spreading their fame; and lastly, the ignorance of the laws governing the transformation of human society."

Ibn Khaldun's observations still ring very clearly in this era of the digital revolution, especially in the ears of Aydoğan Vatandaş, a Turkish journalist based in the United States and the author of several bestselling books. He has long been interested in the evolution of the media and the role it plays in global understanding, especially in the digital depiction and even stimulus of the recent events in the Middle East. In this series of essays with leading figures in the journalism and publishing fields, Vatandaş brings his unique investigative approach and perspective as a journalistic bridge-builder to explore these questions and to seek that middle meeting field of differing cultures and approaches. His interviews shed light on the various ways the US press has reported such topics as the leadership role of Turkey in the Middle East, the death of Osama bin Laden, the role of Hamas, the role of social media in the Arab Spring, Islamophobia, Wikileaks, and the future partnership of Turkey and the United States.

Vatandaş's probing inquiries clarify meaning and context. He questions his interviewees on the role of propaganda in the press, citizen journalism, opinion crafting by both sides, and the intimate relationship between politics and media in the United States. His interviews provide a vibrant account of the real issues faced by journalists, and allow us to read between the lines of the news. The net result is an exciting book which delves into the heart of current affairs. We come away from it with a better understanding of the complexity of the political framework in which we live, and how our perception of it is handled by modern journalists in their ardent search for reporting excellence. Vatandaş reminds us that writers must come together in that middle field to stand—along with their readers—in the shadow cast by Ibn Khaldun's wise counsel, to voice human understanding, and to mediate a hope-filled transformation of human society.

Katharine Branning is the author of Yes, I Would Love Another Glass of Tea: An American Woman's Letters to Turkey.

Introduction

Paul Moses

As a young reporter working for the newspaper *New York Newsday*, I covered a trip our city's mayor took in 1987 to Poland and Hungary, which were then under repressive Soviet control. Mayor Edward I. Koch, who thrived on controversy, decided to hold a news conference in Budapest for the local press. He told the three reporters traveling from New York that he wouldn't take our questions; this press conference was for the Hungarian media.

Speaking at a meeting room in a hotel on the Danube, the mayor gave a brief opening statement, and then, his eyes twinkling in anticipation of the give-and-take that would follow, he called for questions. None were posed. Mayor Koch cajoled and coaxed until finally, one reporter stood, and after a flowery, respectful preamble, apologetically asked a mild-mannered and forgettable question. It was clear that the reporters, accustomed to government control of the media, were not going to ask a challenging or even remotely interesting question. The mayor had a crestfallen look on his face, for life without engaging conversations is dull indeed.

In this book of conversations, there is not a dull moment. Investigative reporter Aydoğan Vatandaş asks the right questions—probably the single most important ingredient for good journalism—in a concise and thoughtful way. As a result, his guests offer absorbing insights into a range of topics, from the vast changes in the media landscape to the Arab spring, and to Turkey's role in international diplomacy.

If one theme stands out for me from these varied topics, it is of standing at the crossroads. New York, where some of the interviews were conducted, is a crossroads, home to the United Nations, harbor for immigrants, and a magnet for international finance. A crossroads is a good place for a journalist to be, and Mr. Vatandaş takes advantage of this position by interviewing individuals such as Robert Thomson, editor-in-chief of *The Wall Street Journal*, who discusses Rupert Murdoch's role at the paper; *The New York Times* reporter Anthony Shadid,[1] who gives a riveting account of his being captured in Libya; and Pamela Steiner, a senior fellow at Harvard and great-granddaughter of the US ambassador to the Ottoman Empire in 1915, who tells of how she is working to reconcile Turks and Armenians.

Turkish readers will find it interesting to see how influential Americans view their homeland and its growing importance on the international scene. For my part, I was intrigued by the questions Mr. Vatandaş asked because I think they reflect the same mix of admiration and skepticism about America that his Turkish readers would have. For example, I am proud that the United States has what I regard as the world's most expansive protection for a free press, which, I believe, is crucial in a democracy. But his questions consider a number of shortcomings in the American news media as well, including what one interviewee points out as self-censorship.

Through these interviews, Mr. Vatandaş becomes a sort of intermediary between Turkey and the United States, instructing the peoples of both countries about each other. It seems appropriate to me that an accomplished journalist from Turkey would take this role, since Turkey itself has emerged as an important mediating influence in dealing with some of the world's most difficult problems. Good conversations can be part of the solution.

> *Paul Moses is a Pulitzer Award winner journalist and*
> *professor of journalism at Brooklyn College.*

---

[1]   We lost Shadid before this book came out (February 16, 2012). Shadid could not survive a fatal asthma attack while reporting on Syria.

Preface

Aydoğan Vatandaş

I was born in a suburb of Istanbul in 1974. My family was a middle class Turkish family who migrated from Macedonia in early '60s.

I started my primary education in 1980 in one of the schools in my neighborhood. Even though I was only 6 years old, the year "1980" has always remained in my memory in a very special way. One day, early in the morning, I saw soldiers in every corner of the streets announcing that it was forbidden to leave our houses until a next command.

My father told me that it was a military coup. A military coup? What was that?

I instantly asked my father what the military coup means as a very curious little boy.

The only thing I remember he said was: "It is something good, son. They came to protect us from the Communists!" "Who are the Communists, dad? I asked afterwards.

"They are the atheists, son! They don't believe in God."

"Are they bad people, dad?"

"Yes, son. They are bad people!"

After a while, we heard some noises and screams. The soldiers were in our building. All I understood was that there was supposed to be one of those Communists in our building, too. We learned that he was Mr. Celal. The soldiers arrested him immediately without any hesitation.

I asked my father:

"Is Mr. Celal one of those bad people, dad?"

He said: "No son, he is a very kind person, there must be a misunderstanding."

But there wasn't a misunderstanding. He was a Communist and nobody in the building knew that he was. Later we learned that he was sentenced to 5 years in prison. When he came back from the prison, he set up a grocery store just beneath his apartment. In summers, during the vacations, I used to work in that grocery for Mr. Celal with a great curiosity of this suspicious man. One day, I asked him what Communism was. He didn't answer. Besides that, he never, ever talked about politics or religions during the summers I worked for him. Years later, I saw a movie about the torture in the prisons during the Coup years. I understood why he was still scared of talking about politics at that time.

Therefore, my childhood passed with great curiosity about politics and religion.

My father was a proponent of the right wing and a passionate supporter of the military. In our room, I remember that we had all the photos of the coup leaders and, above all, Mustafa Kemal Ataturk, the founder of Turkey who had a military career as well.

So it is very understandable, I think, why I wanted to be a cadet. According to my father, military was the real power in Turkey and I had to be one of them.

In 1988, I attended the Turkish Naval High School, which was founded in 1773 during the Ottoman Empire.

In 1995, I attended the Naval War College. Day by day, I was being aware of the fact that I actually wanted to become something else and it was absolutely not a navy officer. Sometimes, in life we have to make choices which shape our entire future. I resigned from college in 1995 just to become a journalist.

I was very lucky, and right after I quit the Naval War College, I started working at the weekly news magazine *Aksiyon* and later enrolled at Fatih University to study English literature. It was so fascinating that my military background helped me a lot in my journalism career. I started to cover stories on defense and military-politics relations.

A year later, in 1996, I published my first book titled *Armageddon*, about the US foreign policy in the Middle East and its influence on Turkish interests in Iraq. Because I used some classified documents, I was brought to trial by the Turkish military for this book, but was later found innocent.

In 2000, I started to write for the daily *Zaman* and a year later, I graduated from Fatih University.

I had an unprecedented desire and ambition to write new books and new stories. Since then I wrote several other books in Turkish many of which were best sellers in Turkey.

In 2006, I was assigned to work in New York as a correspondent for my news organization. Later on, I noticed how lucky I was to find new people to interview from the other side of the world. As a Turkish journalist, I strongly believe that the interviews I had in the US with my counterparts and some scholars were very important for not only my community but for the American people as well. I asked my questions to understand the nature of the recent political and social developments, from their eyes. And by collecting some of my conversations in this book, I wanted to share their ideas with the rest of the world.

As you may notice easily, most of my interviewees are in the news business. I believe that this book may help you to see the nature of media landscape in the US But I also questioned the recent developments in the social media, which appeared after the rise of internet and digital technologies. Take the Arab Spring for example. What was the influence of the social media on the Arab Spring? Did it trigger the developments in MENA (Middle East and North Africa) or is it being overstated? In this book, I am not guaranteeing full answers to these questions, just like no one else can do, but I hope my questions and the answers I got will provide you with some original perspectives.

We are living in an era of huge transitions and geopolitical shifts. This books aims to ask some provocative questions and find out some answers to discover these transitions of our time.

To be honest, I have to note that the American journalists are more approachable than most of their Turkish counterparts. They were more humble than I expected. I would like to thank all my interviewees for this wonderful journey. It was an honor and a privilege for me.

The title of my book, "Reporting from the Bridge," is a gift from Ms. Katharine Branning. I would like to thank Ms. Branning and Mr. Paul Moses for their wonderful introductions to the book.

Aydoğan Vatandaş,
April 2012, New York

Turkey's emergence is not only important but it's a big story as well

Interview with Robert Thomson, Editor-in-Chief of The Wall Street Journal

I am very happy to be one of the first journalists who have interviewed Mr. Robert Thomson, the editor-in-chief of *The Wall Street Journal*, one of the biggest newspapers in the world.

I was very impressed during my interview with him to hear his visions about the future of the print media and the impact of the new digital technologies on the news business. The interview was conducted on September 20, 2009. Here are some highlights from Mr. Thomson:

The future of the paper: "The print version of *The Journal* is going to be around for a very, very long time. The doomsayers are just wrong, completely wrong. Our sales are increasing and they're only increasing because of the reason you mentioned—serious political coverage, serious international coverage, serious science and health coverage is in decline. There just aren't as many specialist journalists writing about those things in newspapers. There's an opportunity here."

On Rupert Murdoch: "Rupert is passionate about newspapers, he's passionate about news. What we are experiencing at *The Wall Street Journal* is the articulation of that passion."

The length of stories: "You all have to ask yourselves how much of the paper do you actually read each morning. It's a question we must ask now. Stories should be faster, quicker and more scoop oriented!"

On the Web site: "*The Journal* is much more conscious of things like search-optimization and much more aware—and we'll begin to institutionalize this in the autumn [2012]—of what should be free and of what should be paid for."

On increasing arts coverage: "We increased the arts coverage!"

It was my pleasure to talk with Mr. Thomson about all these issues and see his vision for the news business in the future.

**What did you say to your employees first at the Wall
Street Journal when you took over as editor?**

Well, first you might recall, when Newscorp. took over the Dow Jones,
there was a lot of reporting about how to a certain extent the Australian
barbarians were not just at the gate but were in the elevator and could
you please stop the elevator. So, there was a lot of controversy, and of
course the temptation in such circumstances is to reassure people. Certainly you don't want to frighten them unnecessarily.

I'm sure some people believe what they read in a newspaper like
The New York Times, I am sure that they were unnerved but at the same
time you want to make them aware of the difficult reality that newspapers and media are generally facing. I think one of the problems in this
country and the world at large has been that journalists themselves, who
are supposed to report on society, have almost been willfully unaware
of the changes in society.

When you pick up an iPhone, you are not just picking up a telephone,
but an information center. And this willful unawareness has made many
media organizations very vulnerable to those changes and you see it for
example in the end of the Christian Science Monitor as a newspaper, the
trouble in Detroit, San Francisco, Denver, Seattle and many other papers
around America, and to a certain extent around the world.

So, the initial message had to be that this was a time of great challenge and we have to be smart and confront that challenge but if we do
so with intelligence, creativity and professionalism then it's a great
opportunity for us. So I think that message, thanks to the support we get
from News Corporation and Mr. Murdoch, has been shown to be a fair
one. The potential that the Dow Jones and the Journal has is beginning
to be realized.

I think for the last six months of circulation as reported not just by us
but the Board of Bureau Circulation, which is the official measure of these
things in the US, of the top 25 newspapers only one measured any growth
in circulation and thankfully that one was *The Wall Street Journal*. And
similarly online we now have about 22 to 33 million different people from
around the world come to WSJ.com. On the iPhone app, we have a special
news service. In about three weeks 650,000 people downloaded the app.
Of course not all of these people are using it every day but it just shows

you how much the nature and character of the audience is changing and how much the same must change in regards to the content.

So that was both the initial message and the continuing message to the staff. If you remember the Journal from two years ago and you were looking for international coverage, some days there would be only one or two stories. Whatever the economic upheaval we find ourselves in the midst of now, one thing is for certain, globalization is not going away, it is still changing the world. It is more important that readers, professional people, and average citizens understand this world. To understand your context is to understand that it's a global context. So we created extra space in the paper, you will see now that we have an international section that is often 4 to 5 pages and it appears every day.

One of the other things that we know is that there are sophisticated readers in America interested in the rest of the world and so we see that as an opportunity, and frankly one of the things we are doing now is that we have appointed a correspondent in Turkey. We did not have one before. But he is in the midst of moving and starting to report. Clearly Turkey is an important story; economically, politically and culturally. With all the issues going on in Europe and its role in Turkey, these are big important themes. One of the problems in America is that there isn't enough reporting on Turkey. We see this as not only an informational and editorial opportunity but clearly Turkey is increasingly important culturally as well. We see it as a legitimate opportunity.

The paper has moved towards more of a scoop form of journalism, do you think that this strategy will work?

Yes, but it's an interesting question. The Journal has long stories. It can be characterized jokingly as looking at the world from 30,000 feet with 30,000 words. Not many people have the time to read 30,000 words everyday or even in a week. So we felt that WSJ was a newspaper and should have news rather than just features. One of the problems we foresaw in features is that, if you kept emphasizing features rather than news then you are in effect taking away a reason to read the paper every day. I think that you need to pick up the paper and feel like that there is something that you need to read.

The news itself though should be reported differently than anywhere else because we pay specialists to focus on a certain subjects or countries and you can imagine that the WSJ's quality of news will be very high due to our level of access to leaders in the business world. So the quality of our news even if it's on a familiar subject should be uniquely good which is what we aspire to provide. But it is fair to say, which is implicit in your question, that some journalists felt that the uniqueness of the Journal would be lost if we focused on news. However what you have to keep reminding people, and frankly I have to remind myself, is that the WSJ needs to be uniquely valuable to the reader. Journalism is not written for journalists, it's written for readers. So unless it has a purpose and functionality in a readers' life, they will stop reading. Thankfully so far, the opposite has happened.

Does this investment strategy cost a lot?

No it doesn't. With Dow Jones we are able to repurpose the content in so many different places and in different formats. So for example if we wrote a story about Turkish telecoms, it might appear in the paper, it will appear on the web. If it is a scoop we can put it onto newswires. People pay more for newswires than they do for the paper. The story might be about Turkish economic growth, because that is an important figure for the world, we have what they call an algorithmic news service whereby it's not in words but in computer code so we translate it directly to computer format which talks to a computer in an investment house or proprietary trading desk environment. So we are able to charge and monetize all these various formats that the news could be in. I think we are pretty confident that the investment in content is not just of journalistic or social importance but also commercial value.

Your website looks more readable and more relevant. What was your strategy in this regard?

To make it more readable and relevant. But seriously speaking, people look at a website and a newspaper in a different way. If you think about a newspaper, it's a landscape, you survey it. But with a website it is more hierarchical. You scroll it rather than looking at it in a different format and actually it is a different skill. So for example if you take the headline feed, if you have a Blackberry or an iPhone, only a small percentage of people actually read the story. They just look at the headlines. About 10% read the paragraph and only a few percent read the story. So you have to understand how people interact with the medium and one of the key ways is to keep the content fresh, make the site constantly live.

So we put quite a bit of pressure to make people file more stories. First of all for the newswires, we charge commercial clients for the newswire and then obviously we charge for the web as well. What I have noticed coming over from London, when you go to a newsstand over there, there are about 15 national newspapers and it is extraordinarily competitive. Which you could say brings out both the best and the worst of journalists. But what it does mean is that particularly on the web, the level of competition has brought advancements particularly in terms of search engine optimization—which is about making sure your site has more impact on the web. So we have brought across those lessons learned to New York. The other thing is we are lagging a bit behind in the use of audio/visual content; however this is also true of other US newspaper websites.

I remember there was a recent story about gay marriage and it took up more space than any other business news story in the paper. Is this due to your competition with The New York Times *or are you just beefing up your coverage of social issues as a whole?*

I'm not sure about that particular story or that particular day. But generally it is fair to say that we are competing with *The New York Times*. I think there is an opening around America; their national edition is quite vulnerable. And frankly I think their Washington coverage is skewed, and so coverage that has as its objective of being objective, there is a real value for us. In areas like broad national coverage, art, health—all of these things are of interest. But at the heart of the WSJ are the B and C-section, business and finance. Whatever else we do we will not be lessening the importance of our financial and business coverage.

What is the biggest challenge you are facing since you've started?

Revenue. I mean it's been fascinating to watch the collapse that is going on Wall Street. But when your readers are getting fired that's probably not good for the business, when your advertisers, Bear Sterns, Lehman Brothers, are no more that is clearly not good for business. That has been far more challenging than anyone could have anticipated. On the other hand the scale of the opportunity we have, not just in America but globally, when people think of the Dow Jones they tend to focus on the *Wall Street Journal* but it's comprised of other products like MarketWatch that we have been able to leverage in terms of specialty and focus.

I think people are quite fascinated with Mr. Murdoch,
how does he actually impact the paper? What do you
generally talk about with Mr. Murdoch?

We generally talk about the world. I mean his range of interests is extremely broad and his level of curiosity and energy is virtually endless. And that is a good thing because it puts me on notice. We have shared interest in British politics. We talk about China a lot. The future of the media is another topic of discussion, Wall Street ... So his interests are broad, he's enthusiastic and supportive, I mean if you had a proprietor who wasn't interested in what you were doing, I think in the end that would be negative not only on me as an editor but on all of the business. Because it is not only the relationship that I have with him but all those around who work with him that are affected. His attitude has a profound impact on the work they do. They believe they are working for someone who is passionate about media.

You have investments in Turkey, right?

Well Newscorp. does and to be honest I am probably not the person to ask about those things. But I think it is definitely true that the company recognizes the importance of Turkey. There is interest in Turkey's development. The *Times of London*, if you read the editorials, frankly I was very strongly of the opinion that Turkey should join the EU and was quite critical of Germany. The French position was a little vague but possibly not that different. In terms of global development Turkey's emergence is not only important but it's a big story as well.

What does Turkey mean to you? Because of your
Australian background, I know that for many Australians,
Turkey is kind of a pilgrimage.

That's very true. I haven't been personally but that is something I would quite like to do with my children who are sort of Australian. My children are half Chinese, born in New York but raised in London. So they will be able to choose what they like when the time comes. But I think the point you raised is very true, because of Gallipoli and the First World War. All

Australians grow up with that life story and the recognition of that moment and also frankly recognition of the great character of the Turkish people. There is a genuine respect for the people of Turkey.

What do you think about the Turkish government?

I honestly don't know. I have met Mr. Erdoğan several times. I think partly, and I say this as someone who works for an international company, how you internationalize and create local competition so that you have standards that meet and beat the rest of the world is important. You should have every reason to believe in the confidence of your ability to do so. But it means that you have to open up to a certain extent, and clearly that is politically sensitive. In the end the outcome is no doubt beneficial, but if you look at the problems Japan has had coping with the outside world, you have to be careful. On the one hand they have been really great exporters, but on the social side of business, it has really been a failure. The opportunities for the Japanese people have been limited by their inability to communicate and deal with the outside world. It has been limited because they have been so protectionist.

In the case of Turkey, that doesn't mean that you have to open everything all the time, but it means erring on the side of opening up. But I think it takes a will to have those often-difficult battles with local interests for the sake of the national and international good. So however Turkey is doing right now, and I do not know that exactly, I would have an enormous amount of faith in Turkey's ability to compete economically and for Turkish companies to become some of the best known in the world as they should. But those companies will only be able to do so if they are fit for competition on the global stage.

Captive in Libya: "I thought we might be shot in the head!"

Interview with Anthony Shadid, The New York Times

An American reporter was shot and wounded in the shoulder in Ramallah in 2002 where Israel warned that foreign journalists were at risk and should not be in the occupied West Bank city.

He was Anthony Shadid, a Washington-based Boston Globe reporter on an assignment in Ramallah at that time. He was standing in a doorway of a shop with Globe stringer Said al-Ghazali when he was shot. He was hospitalized with moderate injuries.

9 years after that incident, Anthony Shadid along with four other journalists was captured in Libya in March by Militia forces loyal to Muammar Gaddafi. They were held for nearly a week, during which they were threatened, before ultimately they were released into the custody of Turkish diplomats.

We lost Anthony Shadid on February 16, 2012 after a fatal asthma attack while reporting on Syria. Anthony Shadid was *The New York Times* Bureau chief based in Baghdad and Beirut. He won the Pulitzer Prize for International Reporting twice, in 2004 and 2010.

He authored two remarkable books: *Legacy of the Prophet: Despots, Democrats, and the New Politics of Islam* and *Night Draws Near: Iraq's People in the Shadow of America's War.*

I had conducted an exclusive interview with Mr. Anthony Shadid in May 2011 and asked him about his extraordinary experience during the days he was held in Libya Military Intelligence Headquarters and several other questions arising after the death of Osama Bin Laden.

Can you tell me what you think about the death of Osama Bin Laden? What will be the consequences?

I think it says something about how far the region has come since 2001, but I think more significantly what has happened in the past few months has really kind of inaugurated a new era, in which Bin Laden was becoming increasingly irrelevant to. I think his death was kind of an epitaph, an ending to that era, a kind of symbolic moment in this ten years of terrorism, invasion, war, conflict, where we've actually opened up a new page in the era of the world, that is hopeful, despite what we've seen in some countries. His death, I think, was a marker of that.

Can you explain how this new era will look like?

I think it's still very unclear. I think for a lot of us who came out of covering Egypt and Tunisia were probably almost overly hopeful that these revolutions were so easy in some ways. People died; there was still conflict, but in the end it wasn't the carnage we've seen elsewhere. I think what we're seeing is the more realistic idea of what is ahead. I think the easy revolutions in Egypt and Tunisia are over. The more protracted conflicts, the ones that may be violent, ones that may be very difficult, I think of Libya, I think of Syria and Yemen... We're talking about a process that's going to last months, even years. I think the trajectory is still the right one. I think we are headed toward a healthier, more democratic Arab world, but I think the path to that end is going to take a lot longer than people might have predicted in January and February.

What do you think triggered all these uprisings in the Middle East?

I was talking to my wife. It's remarkable to us how many conversations you had in December, say where people talked about the Arab world at its lowest point ever, where people seemed disappointed, dejected, depressed. There wasn't a lot of hope that any change was going to happen. I think what it needed was a spark, a catalyst that set in that crystallized forces that had been bubbling for years, but hadn't reached that critical mass where they could bring about change.

Let me give an example. In Egypt we had a brief kind of opening back in 2005 [with] the Kabbaya movement that was later crushed, but around that time you had people organizing around women's rights, youth, labor—labor most importantly. You had a space for the opposition in Egypt, the growing anger and disenchantment with the reforms for the wealthy class, while the poor were getting poorer. And in the most general terms you had a state failure, a state that wasn't able to take care of its citizens. That social contract had been in place for over 50 years. I think the culmination of all these things together created a revolutionary climate that needed a catalyst. I think, as superficial as it may sound, Tunisia was that catalyst.

Do you think the impact of the social media is being a little overstated or did it have a profound impact?

I think when you put social media in the context of all media it does have a place in that. If we talked about social media on its own I don't think it was a decisive factor in these Revolutions. Did it have an impact? Absolutely. Egypt, Libya, Tunisia, these revolutions were furthered in some ways because of social media. But I think you have to put social media in the context of Al Jazeera and other Arab satellite networks. Without that combination of both, Tunisia may very well not have happened. And I think once Egypt happened it was inevitable, but was it sped up because of the social media? It might have been sped up, but I think it would have happened with or without social media.

How do you think Al Jazeera changed the public sphere in the region? How did it work?

Its access. I think that's the first, the bottom line. Al Jazeera was able to turn an audience what might have been social media audience of millions to an audience of tens of millions or even hundreds of millions. I think, especially early on, Al Jazeera had a very canny sense of what the conversation or discussion is with its audience. If you watched the way it packaged the Revolution in Egypt as it was going on, it understood its readership and the way it resonated with its viewers. And it was very powerful. There were moments when you would hear songs by Umm Kulthum. Poetry sung by Sheikh Imam. To an Arab audience these resonated with a sense of reclaiming a lost past. It was very effective.

I think its role has changed since then, I think it's fallen victim particularly [to] pressures of its owners in Qatar and the Saudis. Its coverage has been much less ambitious when we think about Bahrain for instance or even the change going on inside Saudi Arabia, or even the

Gulf for that matter. They've been aggressive about Libya, Yemen and Syria, but these are easy targets in some ways because there's not been a lot of Saudi or Gulf anger about what's going on there. When it comes to the change in the Gulf itself, it has not done a lot as well.

Why do you think these uprisings didn't work in Algeria for example?

To be honest, I don't really know the answer. I think after Tunisia happened, people were really expecting Algeria to be the next theater of dissent, change and uprising. To be honest I really don't know the answer to that. It's early—we have to keep in mind it has not been much since this all began. I think it's a years-long process. Algeria may very well go in the same direction, months from now, years from now.

Let's go back to Egypt. Do you consider this as a revolution or a military coup?

That's a great question. To me right now, I think you're right to be cautious about the use of the word "revolution." I think we have to see where this ends up in a year or even five years. Was it a military coup? There's something grander than that though. While it may be hard to call it a revolution at this point, it's not right to call it only a military coup. Without the military stepping in this it would be much more of a protracted conflict but the military didn't step in until you had a popular mobilization. We are talking about millions who took to the streets to use protest as a method of change. It was a revolutionary action. That might be the best way to describe it. It's a revolutionary action that's yet to emerge as a revolution that qualifies it as something more than a coup.

Do you think the Muslim Brotherhood will have a say in the democratic system in Egypt afterwards?

To me, the most fascinating element of all these revolutions and uprisings is that very question. What is going to be the emerging relationship between political Islam and the state? And we can't underestimate the influence of Egypt on the region. So many of these currents, ideologies, perspectives, have started in Egypt and spread to the rest of the Arab world. Now Egypt has lost the weight that it once had in the Middle East; I think there is a sense there that it wants to reclaim it. I think these debates that are going on in Egypt today, what role will the Muslim

Brotherhood play? Will there be other Islamist parties that will be part of the mainstream? What rules will they have to play in the emerging political system? How will they function with other political parties, will they create coalitions or go on their own? All these questions that I think will be answered in the next year will have far reaching repercussions on the Arab world. I have to say I'm very optimistic about it. It's a long overdue reckoning and a way somehow reaching a new accommodation between political Islam and the state.

Do you think the Muslim brotherhood will take AKP in Turkey as an example?

It's remarkable how many people in the Arab world have said "If we can follow the Turkish model, we can have a vibrant democracy, a way to incorporate into the mainstream our Islamist currents." I think Turkey is on the minds of every political activist right now, because it is seen as a success story. Can the Muslim Brotherhood become something like the AKP? That's a hard argument to make, only because the brotherhood has had such long history. It remains a rigid movement, it's still burdened a little bit by its past. Could something emerge in the place of the Muslim Brotherhood and try to copy the experience of the AKP? There's one party in particular that's going to be interesting to watch in Egypt—The Hizb al-Wasat— the center party, led by a man named El Amadi, he's been on the landscape for 15 years, his party is legalized. He has a vision that is closer to the AKP then the Brotherhood I think right now. But the question is, can he gain enough following, does he have enough support to be a player in both Islamist politics in Egypt and politics in general.

What do you think will happen in Syria?

It's difficult to see what the end game will be. At the beginning of the uprising, the government was using a mix of concessions and crack-down, and lately it's been much more crackdown. We're not seeing much more efforts for reform on the part of the Syrian government. I think there's a notion there they can end this uprising through force. But you don't know what's going to happen in the long term. What you're seeing right now is a dangerous exacerbation of sectarian tension. You're see-ing a military acting against majority groups, the Sunni groups, the Mus-lims in Syria. This sectarian violence is dangerous. You're also hearing reports that the Sunni business elite in Damascus, less so in Aleppo, is losing a little bit of faith in the government. But I think in the broadest of terms, Turkey is going to have a role in this. Turkey perhaps has the greatest influence in Syria at this point. So what I think Turkey pushes this government to do is going to have a lot of influence.

And do you think Turkey has influence in Iraq as well?

I think Turkey has more influence across the region than what people realize. I think in Iraq I was struck, when I was working on a story about Turkey's reach in Iraq, you can make the argument that Turkey has more influence than Iran or even the United States. And it's because it's seen as, I think, Turkey's approach is a very sophisticated one. I think it's seen as soft power in lot of ways. There's an incredible amount of influence it has through its economic presence, through the trade across the border, through businessmen operating from Erbil to Basra. It also has a diplomatic presence that has remained very open minded. While the Americans will not talk to the Sadrits, while the Iranians have difficulty talking to the Sunni parties—Turkish diplomats are able to talk to everyone from the Sadrists to the Malikies to obviously [the] Alawies who sees them as their allies. It's remarkable to see how Turkey transformed its role in Iraq in the past few years; it's almost unrecognizable when you compare it to 10 years ago.

Can you tell me what happened in Libya nd how Turkey had access to Libyan military intelligence service and rescued you? And tell me your recollections with the Turkish diplomats?

Our biggest fear when we got arrested was that no one was going to be able to help us, that no one would know where we were and how to get us out of there. And no one really did for the first few days. And almost immediately when we got to Tripoli we got the sense that the situation had changed. We were abducted on Tuesday and we got to Tripoli by Thursday night, and I think Friday morning we had our first meeting with Libyan diplomats and it was made clear to us that the Americans were not going to be able to do anything, the British were not going to be able to do anything—Turkey was working on behalf of Britain. So our British colleague was able to have some kind of diplomatic representation. It lasted over 36 hours, Americans had to wait and see if Turkey

would accept their diplomatic role. Had it not been for the Turkish diplomats I think we would very possibly still be in custody. The Libyan
government insisted that an American diplomat had to come and pick us
up on Friday. The Americans refused of course, they had already started
bombing at that point. The Americans wanted us to be driven to the border and dropped off, but Libya was not going to accept that. At least they
wanted the pretense of having a diplomatic exchange. And that's where
Turkey came in. I have to say I've been very impressed with Turkish diplomats in Iraq and Syria and elsewhere since I've been working in the
region. I was impressed with them in Tripoli as well and they knew how
to handle themselves. They understood the culture and they understood
the importance of a certain diplomatic respect, and you could tell that
Libyans appreciated their presence very much. The Turkish embassy
was called three or four times. I think the first time was [on] Saturday,
Saturday night, and Sunday morning, I think three times. Each time saying to come and pick us up but we were never dropped off. And finally
on Sunday they called the Turkish diplomats, met us at the headquarters, the ambassador and two other diplomats and the exchange was
made there. We were put in cars and taken to the Turkish embassy and
the minute I stepped in the Turkish embassy, I knew that I was going
home. It was a very good feeling.

Did you say the Turkish diplomats started that initiative on behalf of the British diplomats?

So at the very beginning Turkey was taking care of British interests in
Libya after the Brits had closed down their embassy. They weren't doing
the American interests, only after our case came up and they couldn't
figure out how to make an exchange, the Americans asked the Turks to
take care of their interests.

What happened to your driver?

We're still trying to find out about that. Our fear in the beginning was
that he was killed because we didn't see him after we were seized that
evening or that afternoon. When we were seized, there was a very big
firefight or gun battle and we didn't see our driver after that, so our
fear was that he might have been killed. But we've been following up
since then and a journalist for *The New York Times* went into Libya to

find out his whereabouts. We've heard rumors that he may be in custody. But to be honest after all these weeks, there's no conclusive word whether he's alive or not.

What did you feel when you were first caught by the
Libyan soldiers? Were they intelligence soldiers? Did you
feel you may die, for example?

I did, we were picked up at 4 pm in the afternoon and that first night I thought there was going to be a good chance that we may die. We were picked up by militia. It wasn't really soldiers and they were dressed ragged. Equipment wasn't all that good. It was clear that there were part of some military, but they felt more like militia and an army. And when they threw us on the ground one of them said in Arabic "Shoot them!" And his colleague said, "You can't, they're Americans." And that was the closest it came, we were lying on the ground and I thought we might be shot in the head. But we weren't. And in that entire night what was scary was that there were gun battles going on every hour or so between the rebels and this militia we were with. We were worried the whole time we would be caught in the crossfire.

What did you feel when you won the Pulitzer Prize for the first time?

Of course, the happiest moment was the birth of my daughter and son. But I have to say winning the Pulitzer the first time ranked up there. I was in Baghdad at the time, and it was a very difficult time, where fighting had become much worse. You're obviously happy about winning the Pulitzer Prize, but it's more the work you did there that had some impact. People were reading it, that people cared to read it and think that was really worthwhile. I think a lot of these stories are frustrating when it feels like no one really cares about them and Pulitzer was in some way recognition that people did care about the stories.

And Osama Bin Laden, do you think the way he was
buried in the sea was a little bit suspicious?

Americans would understand that there would be suspicion about that. I think you're right. And I think a lot of people in the Middle East are questioning that. Are they trying to hide something? Was it really Bin Laden? I'm sure they're tying to prevent the idea of a shrine or a pilgrimage or something like that. But if that was the case, they could have buried him in Saudi Arabia. There would be no shrine there; it would be a very simple grave. You know it probably was a mistake, to be honest. One, I think it offended religious sensibilities. Two, it raised suspicion that wouldn't have to be there necessarily.

Do you think the celebrations in New York and also Washington was a bit patriotic? I know he was a mass murderer and that he was a terrorist, but do you think it's appropriate to celebrate someone's death in that way?

You know that's a good question. And I think a lot of people have raised that point. Why all these celebrations and we're still talking about death? I think Arabs are often criticized for celebrating death when it happened. Why do you celebrate this? Was it a moment for the United States that's hard for us to understand abroad? It rubbed a lot of people the wrong way in this part of the world.

There was an initiative called the Broader Middle East Initiative, it came out just after September 11 by the Bush administration. Do you think that there is a relation right now, to what is happening in the Middle East, North Africa and that Greater Middle East Initiative? Because we know that in 2008, the State Department invited some of the representatives of these youth movements to New York to discuss several issues about the usage of social media. Do you think the United States is in this game?

You know the broader policies of the Bush administration probably delayed the Arab Spring. I think the invasion of Iraq was a disaster. You know it destroyed that society and it created a level of carnage and violence in some ways I think the Arab world is still reeling from. I also think the Arab Spring was inevitable with or without American help. And it was the forces that we saw in Egypt for instance, labor activists, youth activism, women's rights, political opening for opposition, growing frustration with the government—all these things would have led to change eventually. But I think your point is right, I think it's underappreciated that where the Americans spent money on that kind of training did have impact. It's hard not to acknowledge there was influence from these activists, and a lot of them did receive training and financing and they played a part.

*What do you think about Obama's address to the nation after
the death of Bin Laden? Do you think American troops will leave
Afghanistan? How will it affect America's Afghan policy?*

I think it's going to raise questions of how deep and long is the American presence going to remain in Afghanistan, when the very premise of that involvement was in some ways to find Osama Bin Laden. That premise is no longer there. I think you're going to see growing awareness on the part of the American public to underwrite this deep of a military presence in a country in some ways that doesn't have strategic stake. My sense is that we're going to see a shorter-term involvement, rather than a longer-term involvement. I have to say and I feel this pretty strongly, we have begun a new era in the Arab world. It's going to be a difficult one, potentially bloody. We have a lot ahead. But the potential is as vast as any time in recent history for what the Arab world can become—a more democratic place. As a journalist getting to witness this and work on it, it's incredibly exciting.

Turkey is one of the most critical relationships for the US

Interview with Dr. Joshua W. Walker, University of Richmond

D r. Joshua W. Walker is an Assistant Professor of Leadership Studies at the University of Richmond and is currently a post-doctoral fellow at the Crown Center for Middle Eastern Studies at Brandeis University. He is also a research fellow at the Harvard Kennedy School and a non-resident fellow at the German Marshall Fund based in Washington, D.C. His research focuses on the role of historical memories in post-imperial successor states, with a particular focus on Japan and Turkey's domestic and foreign policies. Dr. Walker completed his Ph.D. in Politics and Public Policy from Princeton University with a focus on international relations and security studies. He holds a Master's degree in International Relations from Yale University and a Bachelor's degree from the University of Richmond. He was a Fulbright Fellow in Ankara, Turkey and he has worked for the US Embassy and State Department in Turkey in 2004. In addition to his numerous articles, briefs, and book projects, he has been published in a variety of outlets including *Christian Science Monitor, Foreign Policy, International Affairs, International Herald Tribune, New Republic, Washington Quarterly*, and *Washington Times*.

I interviewed Dr. Joshua W. Walker about the new Turkish Foreign Policy in the Middle East and the recent developments in Egypt.

When we read the US diplomatic cables released by Wikileaks, we see a lot of criticism about Turkey's new foreign policy. The Foreign Minister Mr. Davutoglu has also been called an extremely dangerous mind. So can you tell us why he has been described in those terms? Secondly, do you think the US vision for Turkey has changed because President Obama has appointed a new ambassador to the country? He called

Mr. Erdoğan and said something to the effect of "we understand your position." So do you think that Obama's administration shares Turkey's new role in the Middle East right now?

I mean this is one of the most fascinating points and I write a lot about the US-Turkey relationship and a lot of my friends think that I am a little bit strange because I focus so much on it. When you think about the world today, why aren't you focusing on US-China, why aren't you focusing on US-India? Those are really important, don't get me wrong, I'm not saying that Turkey is more important but it is one of the most critical relationships.

Because for so long the US has taken Turkey for granted and I think we saw that particularly during the Bush administration where there was a sense of when we ask the Turks to jump, they ask us how high, not whether they should jump or not. But there has been a real questioning in Turkey that asks, what is this relationship about anymore? We understood during the Cold War that you kept us safe from the Soviets, but now what do we do, what's the point of being in a relationship? I think it's incumbent upon the US as both a super power and also as the framer of international order, to illustrate why it is important that democracies work together.

Democracies are messy, as we are watching right now in the region. And Turkish democracy is particularly messy. Anybody who's been to Turkey and who watches it knows this. I mean it's amazing to me, I'm a professor of international relations and I step into a cab in Turkey and suddenly I am being lectured on international politics. Everybody in Turkey is an expert on international politics where as in America (aside from New York taxi drivers) most people do not have an opinion. When I ask my grandparents in rural Virginia what they think about X, Y and Z in the international scene they kind of look at me like and say, "I didn't know that was happening, where is that country." But in Turkey everybody has an opinion about America and everybody is a US expert. That makes it very difficult for a democracy to function because the AKP has to be very careful, because if they do anything with the US, it is used by their opponents against them, saying, "These guys are the stooges of the US because they agree with the US."

I think what we saw with the Bush years was a complete breakdown in the relationship. The US was like, "where is the Turkey of the cold war? Where is the Turkey that says we are going to do whatever it takes, we are going to be your tool in the region?" However, the Turks very clearly said "no, we have our own ideas." The Turks I think were really frustrated with the Bush administration. And I think that what we saw, with the coming of the Obama administration, was real euphoria. They were saying, "look maybe this can be different. Maybe one man that has this entire baggage and the entire hopes of one nation can change every-thing overnight." I think 2009 was probably the pinnacle in some ways of Obama's honeymoon period of US and Turkish relations.

Obama went to Turkey and gave probably one of the best speeches I have ever seen. He was able to say things to Turks that even Turks couldn't say to themselves. And he said "look, as a black man in America I am not proud of all of our history, but [it] has made us stronger because of it. You need to look at the mirror and look at your history and realize that you have great potential and the only way we can realize that poten-tial is by working together." I think there was a real sense of things changing, with the Prime Minister coming to this country and the for-eign minister being changed to Davutoglu, who is a professor, and has these very grand views of international relations. By the way, in full dis-closure, he was my professor as well, so there is something to be said about how I objectively look at him but I think it's important to look at that period of time and then the shattered dreams of 2010.

I think that what 2010 has taught us is that it's good to have great leaders that can get along on a personal level but it's more than just about the President and the Prime Minister. There are other factors at work. And I think what we saw in the US was a real sense of Turkey's enemies finding crucial and important ways to poke holes in the rela-tionship. When I look at today, even the fact that the US ambassador to Turkey took 7 months to get appointed, it shows you how sensitive that relationship is. The Republicans in some ways look at Obama and see he invested so much of his time in trying to make Turkey an important country, and think "if we can screw that relationship up it will screw him politically." And so focusing so much on the domestic hurts the foreign policy in the long term and creates a much bigger problem.

When I think about the Wikileaks, the ambassador that I worked for as well, Ambassador Edelman was mentioned a lot and he has a lot of these controversial views. Having worked in the State department, I am torn in some ways because that was for internal consumption. That was supposed to be seen only by certain eyes and just because you write that doesn't mean that is your policy. It takes a lot of sausage to make the sausage product at the end. And what goes through, that process, if you take anyone piece of fat and look at it, it's disgusting, but I think it is important to say "what does the final product look like?"

When I look at US policy towards Turkey, for the most part in the Obama administration it has been good. I would say it looks like it is an acknowledgement of a fellow democracy. But when I look at what is happening on the outside, when I look at the lobby groups within Washington today, when I look at certain senators or congressmen who don't really care all that much about foreign policy issues and they are more concerned with painting Turkey to be this Islamist country to be the next Islamic Republic of Iran. There are some nefarious forces at work there that have nothing to do with Turkey. But it is very hard to convince the Turkish voters of that. The Prime Minister can't get up there and say Wikileaks happened guys, but they are not really insulting us. Actually, I think the way the Turkish government reacted was very interesting; they basically made it a non-issue. The Prime Minister has a notoriously thin skin, so he decided to take issue with the personal statements but I think that this idea of Davutoglu being a dangerous mind and that's the way the US embassy thinks about it is incorrect. Just because somebody in the embassy, perhaps I myself, writes one of these cable doesn't mean anything is going to happen back in Washington. And even when the Secretary of State thinks of something, nothing is going to happen in Washington that is not the way it is done.

So despite the fact we have a bunch of American experts in Turkey helping the Turks understand how actually American policy is made it is still really important. Which is why Turkish Americans, the Turkish Cultural Center, these groups have a very important role to play. Conversely people like me have a very important role in helping our policy makers understand how Turkey works. Because I think right now there is a clear misunderstanding on both sides of the Atlantic. One saying "why aren't you doing this for us?" the other "are you doing it because you have a personal problem with me?" There is a real reactive quality here.

Anytime I think of Mediterranean people, and this is not just Turks, they either think that the world is completely falling on them, the world is ending, or they are the greatest thing in the world/the strongest power in the world. Americans, I think, have this tendency to be so in the middle of the road and so emotionless, that people think you guys don't have any friends and are just about interests. But I think Americans do have emotions some times, as we saw with the Iran vote. These issues in terms of human nature do come into play for them.

As you remember, after the AKP took over in Turkey, the US announced a project, which was called Broader Middle East Initiative. Do you think that this initiative is still on the table? Is it related to what is going on now in the Middle East, Egypt, Tunisia etc? How do you think the AKP's role will affect these countries?

I think it's fascinating to think about this Broader Middle East initiative and I am glad that you are bringing it up. It's a great analogy that is not being written about enough. There was a period of euphoria at this point, remember this was right after the war in Iraq in 2004. It seemed that the real insurgency had not begun yet, there were pockets of resistance but things more or less seemed to be going in favor of the US. The seed of revolution was about to happen. Libya had just given up its nuclear ambitions etc. So there was a real sense of maybe an Arab spring happening, maybe there was a real change. However, think about what is being written today in all the newspapers. The Arab world is going to change overnight and it will be a spring and this is the fall of the Berlin wall etc. However, I think there are some differences between this time and that time that we can talk about.

In terms of the Broader Middle East initiative though, because of the messenger, it was dead on arrival. President Bush was not going to be seen as any champion of democracy. Partly because of the way in the US, after 9/11, he had decided to go about things like civil liberties and all the things that were being debated here. But also because of the way he was seen overseas. He was basically seen as a cowboy and as a result no foreigner wanted to stand next to him at all.

It was really interesting when he came to Turkey in 2004, I was a part of that visit, and he gave a speech and said look, we are not having a war on Islam because Turkey is with us. But the discomfort of the Prime Minister of Turkey when he said that was palpable to everyone. It was kind of one of those things where Erdoğan wanted to just hide away. The difference now is everybody wants to be around Obama, everybody wants to be near him and seen. So there is a real difference between even the way Obama has positioned himself.

What's happening in Egypt right now then?

With what's happening in Egypt it would have been very tempting for any US president to get in front of the State Department or anybody else and have a news conference saying, we stand with the protesters and we want Mubarak out. But that would have been very dangerous in a lot of ways. Because of stability and the rule of law, there is no real clear alternative in that region right now. And the Muslim Brotherhood is one potential alternative, which would be much worse from an American perspective or Israeli perspective. That might be what happens and we can have a discussion about that, but the Broader Middle East initiative as it was conceived was to really have America help other countries in the region to be more representative. The idea and the conception of it was a good one and one that I believe continues to live today.

It's funny when I think about Bush and the Neo-cons, who thought they could change the Middle East overnight by toppling one country and yet what has happened with Twitter and Facebook has done far much damage to any Arab dictator than anything any American tank could have done. What is happening right now with the way we are looking at Tunisia as an example and now Egypt as an example seeing how America does and does not respond is critical and I think Turkey's role is critical in this aspect. Because Turkey is the only indigenous player in the region that is a representative democracy and has a conservative Muslim Prime Minister who is popular in the Middle East.

Every poll I see says Erdoğan is the most popular leader in the region. In Turkey though he's kind of got this Bill Clinton charisma to him; either you love him or you hate him. He has this amazing ability to say things in such a colloquial way that really galvanizes the Turkish spirit and he has seemed to tap into something within the Arab spirit as well and I think it's interesting to see that he is saying nothing right now about the conflict in the region. The Prime Minister has more or less said "we want stability in the region." However everyone wants stability in the region, except maybe Iran.

Can you expand on this notion of gain and loss?

The AKP because of its own domestic battles had to be very careful because think if Mubarak crushed this protest movement. If both the Americans and the Turks stood forward and said "we support the pro-testors" and they have now been thrown in jail, are we willing to go in with our tanks to liberate them? Are we willing to take a stand? Or are we going to have the moral ground and say to Mubarak, "we think you shouldn't be as repressive, we think it would be nicer if you let some of this up." So I think the broader Middle East initiative is a great idea that will continue to live. I think Obama is personifying it in some ways but I think the idea is we do not want a "made in USA" stamp on this, I don't think a made in Turkey stamp is good either, it's a lot better than a US one, but I think a made in Egypt, in Tunisia, in Yemen is going to go a whole lot further than anything we can come up with.

I want to ask a question about the Muslim brotherhood in Egypt. In 1998, the Turkish Prime Minister, Mr. Erdoğan, was widely described as an Islamist but since taking office he has totally changed. Sayyid Qutb had an influence on Turkish Islamic movement as well as on Muslim Brotherhood in Egypt. Muslim Brotherhood lived under oppression for a long time and they were never given any chance to be in the governmental system in Egypt. Do you think that if the Muslim Brotherhood were given a way to be in the system they would change? Maybe the US has taken this account; would you agree?

Well that is a hotly debated topic both in the academic and policy world, but I think the general consensus is that as long as there is no alterna-tive to a political solution that holds. The problem is this: Let's take Hamas as an example. Hamas is a genuine political movement. They do a lot of great things in Palestine and Gaza etc. The problem is that when they don't get what they want they resort to violence and I think the same thing can be said about Hezbollah in Lebanon. They are the most politically powerful group in Lebanon right now but what makes them so politically powerful is the army they continue to hold and I think if you resort to that then I think it's going to be an unfair game. Because if every other player does not have its own militia to rise up when things don't go their way you have a serious problem on your hands. What is very interesting about the Turkey example is that the Islamists never kind of resorted to that and that is exactly where Erdoğan comes down on this.

Erdoğan and the AKP have learned a very valuable lesson since and that is basically the idea that they can win politically. The way to win is to abhor violence and be morally above. AKP won in 2002 because they were a new party and they were not corrupt. "AK" in Turkish means white, it means clean, and so when they won in 2007, it was because it was a reaction against the military interference into who would be the president of Turkey. Will the AKP be able to hold that high moral ground going forward? They have been in power for over a decade now and power corrupts. Even the most morally upright at a certain point are susceptible. So it will be important to see what that does to the Prime Minister. To me a scary thought is to think about what Turkey looks like in a post-Erdoğan world. Because even though Turkey is a democracy, it has a tendency to look towards a great man and the AKP without Erdoğan would not be the same and the Muslim Brotherhood has never been allowed to create that in Egypt.

US can learn many things from Turkey in the Middle East

Interview with Tony Karon, Senior Editor of Time Magazine

Turkey, like other countries in the region, was affected by the release of documents. Erdoğan's office said in a statement on its website that President Barack Obama called Erdoğan and told him some of the comments in the cables do not reflect the view of the current US government and that the US-Turkish alliance is vital. However, Erdoğan reacted furiously to claims relayed in a 2004 diplomatic memo. WikiLeaks' release of US diplomatic cables, needless to say, will have an enormous impact on relations between the United States and the rest of the world.

I interviewed Tony Karon, a senior editor at *Time Magazine*, an accomplished journalist who has been focusing on the Middle East for many years about the so-called shift in Turkish foreign policy and how Turkey was portrayed in the US documents. The interview was conducted on 15.12.2010.

How do you think the political shifts in Turkey that you have mentioned in your writings are portrayed in these documents that were released?

To begin with, I think that what we see in the WikiLeaks documents is a lot of what I call nostalgia—nostalgia for an era that is long past and gone. So you have President Hosni Mubarak suggesting to US diplomats that the United States might actually overthrow the current Iraqi government and restore a dictatorship because that is what the country needs.

You have the Israelis saying perhaps it might be better if General Musharraf was back in power in Pakistan and also obviously expressing all this alarm about Turkey—that Turkey has gone over to the Islamists' side, the Iranian side and so on. You have Saudi Arabia's king supposedly asking the US to attack Iran. What is remarkable about all these things, though, is that if you read the subtext, they are not happening. They are not happening.

The Saudis are complaining, supposedly, "When are you going to do this?" And of course, the answer is probably they are not going to do it. Defense Secretary Robert Gates has made it very clear, the reason the US is not going to bomb Iran is because there is not a military option that makes sense. Gates has said this very explicitly, and I think very courageously. This is not a point of view that is very well exercised in Washington discussion.

Politicians who might be seeking re-election don't really say this sort of thing and of course Gates is not seeking re-election, and he says very clearly that bombing Iran's nuclear facilities, at best, will set back Iran's nuclear program by two or three years. But it will unleash all manner of unpredictable consequences across the region. It will strengthen the regime behind the hard-liners, and most importantly it will make sure that Iran does go ahead and build nuclear weapons—which right now, according the US intelligence assessments and most others, Iran has not yet taken the critical decision to do. It's putting the means to make that decision within reach. Assembling, under the rubric of a civilian nuclear energy program, the means to create a "break-out" option, as it's called (like Japan has) whereby assembling a weapon becomes something that can be done in a number of months rather than 10 years. Gates' argument is a very pragmatic realist point of view, but it's not what some US allies in the region want to hear.

What do you think the WikiLeaks documents reflect?

What I think WikiLeaks is reflecting, both from the questions that are coming to the US and their response to these questions, is that this is not the US of 2001 and certainly not the US of the Cold War, when changing a government in Baghdad at a whim might have been a conceivable option. It might be what is wanted, but in these times it is not a conceivable option, and that is what I think people are reacting to.

So within that schema you think: Where was Turkey in that Cold War schema for the United States? It was a good soldier. Turkey was there in the Korean War and there in the Afghan War and has been pretty much marching lock step with the US for most of the last half century. Yet suddenly, you see these events where a more democratic Turkey, where popular opinion is a lot stronger in shaping what the government is doing, and it is actually breaking with the US strategy.

In 2003, we have the Turkish Parliament voting that Turkish territory cannot be used to attack Iraq. And we see Turkey breaking with the US on the question of Iran and what's the best way to approach Iran's nuclear development. On the question of the Israeli-Palestinian conflict and Hamas, the US remains committed to a view of the region in terms of moderates versus radicals. It's a prism of dividing the region according to those who are on our side and those who are on the other side—which President Bush put as "those who are not with us are against us."

Plainly, that policy is not working.

Turkey is advocating something different. Turkey is looking to build bridges between Iran and Western parties. Turkey is looking to build bridges between Hamas and Fatah. Turkey is looking to reconcile Syria and Israel, Syria and the Saudis, and so on. But it is acting independently. In fact one of the cables very explicitly complains that US has "lost control" in this relationship.

That is a source of anxiety in a lot of the cables.

But also in some ways you can see that it is a positive thing. Even some of the US diplomats are recognizing that there is a lot of value in what Turkey is doing, even the break that Turkey is making. Frankly, it is departing from policies that haven't worked. That, for me, is the takeaway. It's all very well to say, "Oh, you are being disloyal," but sometimes a friend has to say, is this working? Are we getting where we want to get with Iran or the Palestinians, with Israel, with the rest of the region? If not, the question is, are these policies going to change?

I think that Turkey in some ways is creating and presenting a different set of options. That is a source of anxiety but also, I think, if you look at one of the key cables from Ambassador Philip Gordon, he concludes that this (break) is Turkish democracy in action. Turkish government's decisions are being shaped by its population. This is what a democratic Middle East actually looks like, and this is not a bad thing. Turkey is offering a model of economic prosperity and development, a government based on Islamic values rooted in the region, integrating its neighbors from the European side from the Asian and Middle Eastern side, and it's a source of stability. And is that really a bad thing? Should that be a source of anxiety? Not if we are relinquishing the Bush administration's disastrous policies of trying to remake the region through revolutionary means.

When Turkey refers to its historical background, particularly its Ottoman Empire background, we see that the US is a little anxious about this. What are your thoughts on this?

I think in the US probably there is a reaction to the idea that Turkey has ambitions to govern all of its former Ottoman possessions. Obviously, that would be a source of anxiety in the United States and probably in a lot of those countries. But if we take the idea that Turkey has a certain history of managing a very complicated set of relationships across a very wide territory and maintaining hundreds of years of stability, then perhaps that appears in a different light.

When the US was setting up the Coalition Provisional Authority to run Iraq after the ouster of Saddam, there was an anecdote from Noah Feldman at NYU, who was one of the professors who was going to help the US as a constitutional advisor to set things up in Baghdad. He was on the US plane with the first group of experts flying there and he was reading a book on Iraqi history. He said everybody else on the plane was reading a book either about Japan or Germany in 1945.

So, what the US was bringing to Iraq, the expertise it was bringing to managing this very complicated place, was its own distinct history—America's own success stories in Berlin and Tokyo of 1945. And actually some of the reporting suggested that J. Paul Bremer, the viceroy who was in charge of the coalition provisional authority, had a chart on his wall where he had benchmarks of progress based on the occupation of Germany in 1945, and he was checking things off as those benchmarks were achieved. In fact, one of the journalists saw an economic document in which the currency hadn't been changed. So this document about Iraq still had reference to the Reichsmark.

In one of the cables, the Turkish side is claiming that actually what they aim to do in the Middle East is also to reduce the Iranian influence in the Arab street. Do you think this is rational or understandable?

Yes, I think that that is very important. It's only if you view the region as a zero-sum game, either you're on our side or you're on the Iranian side, that it is a problem. It's only if you see the region in those binary terms that it becomes a win for Iran. In fact, I think the foreign minister, Davutoğlu, makes the point in that the regimes the US works with in the Arab world are very discredited by and large by their own populations.

They carry very little credibility, which is why the combination of that, with their failure to challenge Israel, and to challenge the US on enabling policies, makes them very unpopular in the Arab world. These all combine to be a primary reason why Ahmadinejad actually became so popular on the Arab street.

But you can see by the opinion surveys a year after Prime Minister Erdoğan challenged the Israelis on Gaza that Erdoğan had eclipsed Ahmadinejad in terms of popularity on the Arab street as the most popular leader amongst the public. You think to yourself, if the goal is stability, integration, development and so on in that part of the world, who is a better role model? Who do we want those on the Arab street looking up to for a role model? I think it's no contest, obviously.

Turkey has interests that differ from the US in terms of how the Iranian nuclear standoff issue should be resolved, but Turkey's interests are hardly identical to those of Iran.

There is obviously potential geopolitical competition; the Turkish side is clearly aware of it. If the US is basing a strategy for stabilizing the Middle East on the likes of Saudi Arabia, Jordan, Egypt and so on, they are not regimes that seem to have much vitality in them. They are not regimes that have much popular legitimacy, that have much momentum. It is hard to imagine Saudi Arabia as a source of stability in troubled parts of the region over many years, so I think that the point that is made in the cables is correct.

And actually maybe we should think about why Iran's influence in the region has grown so exponentially over the past decade. It is really not that hard to see that the key components of it are: a war in Afghanistan that takes the Taliban enemy away from Iran and a war in Iraq that eliminates its primary enemy Saddam Hussein and an unpopular occupational policy in both countries and an Israeli invasion of Lebanon in 2006 that fails to actually achieve its designed goal.

It's plain to see that this massive investment in force in the region as a means of transforming things in a positive direction has absolutely failed. It has achieved the opposite result. Militarily the US is unrivaled in its means to use force and will be for decades to come, but politically it's in a lot of trouble. So, again, Turkey is an example, and it seems like those cables are saying to the US that you need to spend time thinking about what is working and what is not. You need to deal with the reality of what can be achieved in the region.

If the peace talks do not work, what do you think the
next step of the Obama administration is going to be?

The peace talks are not going to work. You heard it here first. I think that
what we are seeing really is that the current run of peace talks are in
some ways mimicking the rituals of Oslo. The Oslo agreement, though, is
long gone, that moment in history has long gone. In fact, it was rendered
a little absurdly in the photographs. There is one of Obama leading
Netanyahu, President Mahmoud Abbas, King Abdullah and President
Mubarak, and there was almost an identical photo on the same White
House carpet in 1995, with President Bill Clinton with Yitzhak Rabin,
Yasser Arafat, King Hussein and Hosni Mubarak. There is a moment of
comedy in this. The premise of Oslo has been that Israelis and Palestinians in bilateral talks will be able to agree on how to partition Palestine,
how to complete that which the United Nations began in 1947 —the partition plan which was accepted by the Israelis but not accepted by the
Palestinians. The Israelis remade the map very deliberately. In the original partition they were awarded 55 percent of the territory. They ended
up in 1948 with 78 percent of the territory.

On the Palestinian side, Yasser Arafat had very cleverly managed to
reinvent the attainment of statehood in the remaining 22 percent of
what had been British Mandate Palestine, as a revolutionary goal. In
other words, there was a bit of sophistry in that the Palestinian national
movement had been formed on the basis of recovering that which was
lost in 1948, he very cleverly reinvented the national goal as the attainment of statehood. This was around 1988 when the PLO adopted statehood (on the basis of the 1967 borders) as a goal. At some point in his
Cairo speech, in talking about the Palestinians, President Obama says
they have been struggling for 60 years for a state of their own. Well
that's not quite how it's been. That is a bit of fudge of the narrative, but
nonetheless that's now in place.

The United States, I think accepts the proposition of using the '67
borders, but the question becomes whether it actually becomes part of
diplomatic strategy. Frankly, in my opinion, domestic politics here is
such that I would doubt that the Obama administration, looking to
secure its re-election, is going to risk it because it would be extremely
risky to do.

Americans don't trust the press

Interview with Professor Carol Wilder, The New School, NY

I n April 2003, 35 percent of Americans believed that Iraq had weapons of mass destruction (WMDs) while 10 percent were not quite sure. In October 2003, 30 percent were still convinced that there were WMDs in Iraq.

But six months later it was understood that there were not any WMDs in Iraq. How could the Americans have been persuaded to believe such a lie without evidence?

It was *The New York Times*, one of the leading and most prestigious newspapers in the world, which actually convinced the Americans. Professor Carol Wilder says, "this is a quintessential example of what happens when the press fails."

Carol Wilder is professor of media studies at The New School in New York, where from 1995 to 2007 she was associate dean and chair of media studies and film. From 1975 to 1995 she served on the Communication Studies Faculty at San Francisco State University (SFSU) as professor and chair. She was named professor emerita at SFSU in 1996. She also served on the faculties of Oberlin College and Emerson College. I had an informative interview with Professor Wilder about the intimate relationship between politics and media in the US.

Let's start first with your experience of the Vietnam War. How did this war influence your worldview and scholarly path?

Well, there is a popular belief that "the media lost the American war" in Vietnam. That belief has some truth to it but it is certainly something that the American government and the Pentagon believe, so subsequent from Vietnam there have been a lot more restrictions on the press. However, I think it is probably more accurate to talk about the relationship between the press/media and the government. In US history in World

War I nobody was allowed to the fronts. So most of what we know about the war is fiction or semi-fiction, like Hemingway ("A Farewell to Arms"), so the relationship between news media, the government and war probably goes back to time immemorial. In World War II there actually was an office of censorship in the US and the reporters of that time, people like Edward Morrow, they were very much on the home team. There wasn't really much dissention; the Allies had to win this war. So the press, the government and Hollywood worked hand in hand, including a series of wonderful propaganda—or motivational films you could call them—by Frank Capra.

Fast forwarding, Korea is where things began to fall apart a little bit because in the beginning of the war in the '50s, which was a messy, awful period—I mean you can't overestimate how the Cold War influenced Americans' thinking. For example, when I grew up we had to do nuclear attack drills and put our heads under a desk, so there was this tremendous fear of Communism during that period, which is why the US went into Korea without a declared war and initially the government was very open to the press until some of the reporters actually started to report what was actually happening. Douglas MacArthur called them traitors, so subsequently the press and the US government left that war on not such great terms, which was sort of a harbinger of what happened in Vietnam.

Continuing to Vietnam, the US was funding the French and the French had been in control of Vietnam from the middle nineteenth century to 1954, when they were defeated at Dien Bien Phu; the Americans subsidized the latter half of that war and then basically took it over. In 1961, when John Kennedy was first president, there was a small band of reporters in Vietnam, the best known of them was David Halberstam, but there was also Peter Arnett, Malcolm Browne and Neil Sheehan. They were a very small group and there was no censorship either, but they started seeing things happening like helicopters being off-loaded on docks in Saigon and being told that they weren't seeing it, so they began to become skeptical about what they were being told from the government. And even though again David Halberstam had this reputation for being out there—I mean he did make Kennedy angry with his reporting—they were all on the home team also. They all wanted America to win; they thought it was a just cause. So this idea that the press was always dissenting, it doesn't hold up with the facts.

So do you think that this was a failure of the American press in its history?

Failure? I don't know if failure is the word I choose. There is a tricky relationship between the government and press in relation to war. War correspondents are a special breed of people and they have some wonderful books about the topic, the best I feel is Phillip Knightley's, called *The First Casualty*, which is a history of war reporting from the Crimean War to the present. So to answer your question, I'm not sure the press failed in Vietnam; in fact I think that press actually helped to end that war. Later we can talk about Iraq and the press's role then. But early in the Vietnam War—the American war from 1961-67—most of the public and the press was onboard. *The New York Times* went astray in 1955, but for the most part public opinion was in favor of that war even though in 1963 there had been the Buddhist crisis.

How do you think that the photograph of the burning Buddhist monk affected public opinion?

Well you know there is an interesting story about that photograph. It was shot by Malcolm Browne, who was one of the journalists in Saigon at the time, and throughout that year of 1963 there had been Buddhist protests and some had been killed. They had been protesting President Diem, a Roman Catholic, who had been oppressing their religion. Malcolm had gotten to know them pretty well and he had been hanging out at a temple in Saigon and he would get word about things that were happening. He had been told prior to that incident that something important was going to be happening the next day. So he was the one that took the famous photographs, but it was very carefully staged; he calls it "theater of the horrible." Quang Duc, the elderly monk who immolated himself, has become highly venerated. His heart was not burned somehow and in fact in Wei, which is in the middle of the country, there is a pagoda with a shrine and the car that drove Quang Duc down to Saigon to self-immolate. In that shrine there is a picture, one of Malcolm Browne's, on one of the windows of the car. A footnote though, the photograph was not even published in *The New York Times* and it was not a front-page story.

The New York Times, one of the world's most respected
newspapers, did not publish this photograph at all. Why so? Do you
think that there is some kind of self-censorship in the media?

Well, if there is a conspiracy it's a conspiracy of capitalism. Everybody is
trying to make as much money as possible and that is the real conspiracy. Capitalism is very much an ideology.

How does this propaganda model work?

Well there is a relationship between the media, the people and the government even now and the US government has become much more
sophisticated in managing the press since the Vietnam War. I mean subsequent to Vietnam we've had Grenada and a whole host of other conflicts; this Iraq war, with its use of embedding, has been a brilliant co-
optive strategy. You have the journalist going along with the troops
under a set of rules and they become identified with the troops so they
can never be really free to report what's going on and they don't see
much more than the small piece that they are a part of. So the Pentagon
has become very slick at managing the press. Back in 1971, Peter Davis,
a filmmaker who got an Academy Award for his Vietnam documentary
"Hearts and Minds," while working for CBS did a documentary called
"The Selling of the Pentagon," which was a long time ago. CBS was doing
a lot of bold investigative journalism at the time; they don't do that so
much anymore, even on "60 Minutes." You don't see them taking that
many chances. Journalism though has changed a lot, during the '60s and
the early years of Vietnam the line between reporting and opinion was
very clearly drawn. Reporters were not supposed to interpret; they were
supposed to report and that does not seem to apply anymore.

When it comes to the Iraq War, do you remember Judith
Miller's stories about WMDs in Iraq? What is your
opinion of that controversy?

Well, Judith Miller wrote a series of very persuasive essays in *The New*
York Times about WMDs in 2003 right before the beginning of that war
and they were scary stuff. It turned out that Judith Miller was a very well
connected person who had gone to Princeton and had gotten a master's
degree in international relations, had spent time in the Middle East and
was considered sort of an expert in American terms. However, it turned

out that the sourcing for these essays was Ahmed Chalabi, who turned out to be a completely fraudulent source pursuing his own agenda. But since it fit right in with the Bush administration's narrative it worked for her. I think *The New York Times* did apologize years later but they didn't mention any names of reporters.

Do you think that American people trust the press?

The Pew Research team does regular studies on the press and has found their credibility is pretty low. I think only 25 percent of the people have high confidence in the press. Fifty percent believe some of what they read—all of these numbers roughly speaking—but to answer the question I would say no, they don't trust the press. Democrats trust the press a lot more than Republicans do apparently, which is interesting, but I think that people trust different press. People don't care; they just want to get their opinions confirmed. Overall though, trust in press, trust in government is low. It makes you wonder how we function at all.

I was very surprised about the media coverage of the UN's report on the flotilla incident; The New York Times covered that story just as a paragraph on page A12. So it seems this kind of behavior is everywhere, what do you think about this?

I think that this incident is so interesting as it unfolds. The Israeli military put something like 20 videos up on YouTube and one of our colleagues sent us a video that was on YouTube that was probably made by the Israeli military. But it was very well done, very professional, very persuasive. It did not have any source. So you couldn't really think about possible bias if you wanted to deconstruct it. Coverage of this incident internationally as compared to the US would be a very interesting study for someone to do.

You mentioned Facebook, and of course there is Twitter and many other examples. How do you think these "new media" are going to affect the media landscape? Will people have more of a voice?

I think the jury is still out on how these new media are going to influence politics. We know that in the 2008 elections it was huge and Barack Obama marshaled a huge online presence and that's what elected him essentially. It was brilliant in the way that they executed that just like a battle plan. On the other hand in *The New Yorker* there was a piece by Malcolm Gladwell, I don't always agree with him, but I do on this and he was saying essentially that the revolution won't be twittered. The point he was making was that on Twitter or Facebook, the ties that one makes on these mediums are not as strong as ties one would make offline. He compares these to those made during the civil rights movement, where there were tight ties made, and a movement that was built through identification and strong leadership. One point that he highlights that may be considered conservative but I agree with him on is that without some kind of leadership, these online social movements are not really going to go anywhere, just as if they were offline they wouldn't go anywhere for the same reason.

How do you think that the advertising model in the media business affects the objectivity of journalism?

There are certainly many examples of corporate media discouraging reporters from working on stories. However, as a reporter, and you know this yourself, you may begin going to your editor and pitching a story that is really out-of-the-box. However, they respond with hesitancy, but you still do it. Then the next time they kind of discourage you and then you don't do it. The next time you don't even go to the editor. And then it becomes like a dog that is on the leash of a pole, you forget that you are on a leash. There is a self-censorship that happens, you don't even think about doing those types of stories anymore because you have been socialized not to. It's kind of like getting tenure at a university; it's supposed to protect freedom of speech but by the time they get it, they have nothing left to say. They have been so socialized, so compromised by the system that they don't even think that way anymore. This is very analogous to the system reporters deal with. It is all very invisible. The dog does not even try to run away because it does not realize it is on a leash.

Let me ask you another question. What struck you most about Turkey?

Your President Mr. Abdullah Gül's speech in Columbia really struck me. Mr. President quoted Michel Foucault in his speech at Columbia; he is probably the first president to quote Foucault I guess. That actually shows how intellectual a president Turkey has!

New media versus old media: The role of the New Media is overstated

Interview with Professor Sean Jacobs, The New School, NY

D r. Sean Jacobs is currently working on a book on the intersection of mass media, globalization, and liberal democracy in post-apartheid South Africa.

Today, there is an enormous shift taking place at lightning speed in the global media landscape. Everyday, a new generation of consumers is born who will grow up in a digital age that most of us are still struggling to grasp and might even find greatly intimidating. At the same time, new digital technologies—such as iPhones and live Internet streams—and new media platforms—including blogs, YouTube, Flickr and Facebook—are creating a new environment and type of journalism: citizen journalism. The new media are evolving into "social media" that impact not only domestic politics but global politics as well.

I discussed all these issues with a remarkable scholar who is an expert on new media and international politics: Dr. Sean Jacobs.

Dr. Jacobs teaches new media and international affairs at The New School, New York. He is a native of Cape Town, South Africa, and has a PhD in politics from the University of London and an MA in Political Science from Northwest University. He is the co-editor of *Thabo Mbeki's World: The Politics and Ideology of the South African President.*

How can we describe new media and what are the distinctions between new and old media? Keeping in mind Marshall McLuhan's famous saying "the medium is the message," what do you think the message is of the new media?

I think the best way to think about new media is to first discuss what it is. I believe that there is a lot of hyperbole surrounding the term and in many cases its effects have been overstated. Not just for how we communicate, but its impact on politics.

The history of political media

Let me backtrack for a moment. In the last 100 years we have had the development of "professional media," especially here in the United States: the emergence of journalism schools in the 1920s, in the '60s it was the idea that media was to be less partisan, and by the '60s and '70s the phenomenon of "new journalism" characterized by a reporter's subjective observations and driven more by storytelling, with writers like Hunter Thompson at Rolling Stone and Tom Wolfe. At the same time a more activist press (e.g., *The New York Times, Washington Post*) grew interested in uncovering government secrets (the Pentagon Papers, Watergate) that spawned more media personalities like Bob Woodward, Seymour Hirsch and Carl Bernstein. This should also be remembered as the time of the news anchors: Walter Cronkite is the best example.

Sean Jacobs, an expert on new media and international politics, states that "while the Internet has made it more democratic in terms of getting information, it has made it harder to get things to the front of the line." However, new media has "enabled people to organize politically"; new media plays a role in "organizing people in what was called the first Twitter revolution."

In the '80s and '90s a small community still controlled what we consumed in the media. In particular, print journalism had emerged as a medium through which we communicate and talk politics. But in the '90s, with the emergence and consolidation of cable television, there was a free-for-all in political media and a return of partisanship with the emergence of CNN as a global media player and Fox News as a major player in the US media scene. Simultaneously, technology changed as well, which de-centered things—we just don't have the newscasters and writers communicating to us as they don't have a monopoly on the news agenda anymore. There is debate and response. This first generation of new media usage allowed us to take these political debates online and make them a little more interactive. As a result, one of the major changes with the emergence of new media has been that it has allowed for a greater dialogue in media communications.

The ascent of the "new media"

I remember in 1995, when the Internet became more of a popular medium, you began to see these crude websites in which existing media started migrating to the Internet. Over time web blogs started to emerge. Incidentally, the most prominent blogs turned out to be by journalists who had grown frustrated with the shortcomings and direction of their profession. The real explosion of blogging by the "blogger in the basement in pajamas" writing about domestic policy and also international policy and educating the US really emerged in the early 2000s.

So when speaking of new media as it relates to political media there is this instantaneous element—an element of being able to directly comment. It's definitely democratic; it has increased the number of voices we hear on a topic. Michael Massing at Columbia University wrote a piece about the characteristics of new media that are very helpful in making these changes. He posits that it also helps with specialization. So if you are interested in a particular kind of topic, let's say tracking political developments in Iraq or those between the Israelis and Palestinians, there are a number of websites that you could go to. You can now read Jeffrey Goldberg (Atlantic Monthly), you can read Juan Cole (professor of history at the University of Michigan, where I used to work), you can read Israeli newspapers online or "electronic intifada." So what it's done is to make available all these avenues to you. But it also means there is some kind of specialization going on. The trouble begins when you realize that now those people are reading only within the small set of voices.

What about the social aspect of the new media?

With the second generation of the political new media there is a social media aspect of things. For example, in the evolution of the use of Facebook, you now may not even go to these specific sites directly anymore. You are now waiting for a friend of yours to update their status to say that Jeffery Goldberg has a piece in the Atlantic Monthly or that Juan Cole has a piece that you should check out. So that small group of individuals I mentioned in the beginning who were so influential do not now have as much control over what we read and how we read it anymore; but a new group—aided by social media—take that function. So the danger is we read less and less widely and more directed stuff. But at least we can read it alongside other sources if we want to. A final point I want to make is that beyond just reading, new media has enabled people to organize politically. There is this argument and I know it's overstated, but it's that new media plays a role in organizing people in what was called the first Twitter revolution. This was applied to Moldova and the same argument was applied to Iran. And of course the biggest one was here in the United States with the election of President Barack Obama.

This is a new phenomenon. Isn't it?

Again particularly in the case of Iran and Moldova, these things are over-stated. In Iran there has been research showing that inside the country it was a very small group of bloggers who were tweeting. Their tweets were in turn picked up outside Iran and then got re-tweeted. And so what we think is millions of Iranians tweeting is in fact the work of often a very small group of people whose works get spread around the world. The second element is there is also other tweeting going on in Farsi. I mean the idea that Iranians are only tweeting in English is silly. And so observers of that uprising overstated the impact of Twitter or they for-got to notice that the government is also organizing online—that they also know about the Internet and also understand its power. So there is a way that these things get overstated in which we make assumptions that everybody is on Twitter, everybody is on Facebook. But these are very small groups of people particularly in the West and particularly in the US. In Britain, for example, the election of David Cameron was the first election where bloggers played a role in the political scene. There is a blogger called Guy Fawkes who became the most prominent blogger in England, but only within this election. But British politicians are pre-tending to use Twitter. They are not really using it in the way that I think it has been used in American politics. I think when we talk about new media we often overstate the use in some of the first world, and if it's in developing countries it's very much a very small set of elites.

Just last week I remembered that there was an Iranian blogger who was sentenced to a number of years in prison, so is there any media activism about this issue?

Well I think what the Internet does is to filter out things. If you look at *The New York Times* online and take a look at the right hand column you will see the there is a section called the most read items. If for example your story—whether it is for example about this Iranian blogger—does not make it to that most read section, what will happen is that it will tend to fall by the wayside. Because increasingly, what is happening is that people will head to these types of sections to see what is important to read. More and more people are reading on their phones, and they check these types of trending items, news stories, that filter to the top and are readily accessible to be read. The way new media is structured is around hits and views, and if a story is not trending or an issue is not trending then people will not be aware of it outside of those who care about those particular issues. Celebrities in this regard dominate online spaces like Twitter and even places like the *Huffington Post* because of their popularity and the structure of new media itself. It's about getting attention. While the Internet has made it more democratic in terms of getting information, etc., it has made it harder to get things to the front of the line.

How does one become a successful blogger? You have mentioned the Atlantic Monthly, where Andrew Sullivan has a popular blog. Is it true that President Obama considers Sullivan's blog a daily must-read? What do you think is the secret of his success as a blogger?

On Sullivan, apart from being a journalist he also has his politics, which is quite out in the open. He used to be a conservative and now he supports Obama. He has an obsession with Sarah Palin, etc. On The Atlantic Monthly site, he is the most popular blogger at this point and during the Iranian protest it was said that the fact that a lot more people cared about the topic in the country could be ascribed to him. He blogged about it and people went to his site because he would take updates from Twitter and people would e-mail him stuff. But I think what makes him successful, and I think this says something about the new media environment, is that firstly it's about irreverence. He will now and then write a very long essay stating his opinion about a topic, but apart from that he is an aggregator. He mostly has one line about something and then will say "read it." Or he will cut and paste a paragraph and have a link from a news story or an article or something. If a reader sends him something he will post it and by posting their e-mails he is creating a community. He's making his readers think that they are a part of the site. He will never mention the actual names of the readers who have sent him comments but it creates a community nonetheless. Secondly, in a piece titled "Why I blog" that appeared in the Atlantic Monthly last year he writes about how blog writing is "writing on the fly." When you write it, it goes out and it's also about engaging with your readers, so the readers might say something and you can respond to it changing your mind and you will write the next day and adjust your opinion on that particular subject. So what's made him successful is not to be rigid about it. He also understands the way that the online news cycle works. That you have to get stuff up Eastern Standard Time between the hours of 8 a.m. and 5 p.m. because that's when people most read their information and want new stuff, within the working hours. So to sum up I think what makes somebody like Sullivan successful or how you become successful at blogging: there is a certain level of irreverence, being timely, a lack of rigidness in the writing itself, a community spirit.

What can you say about the impact of the new media on politics?

In the past there used to be what was called the "CNN effect" on politicians, which was the phenomenon of the 24-hour news cycle pumping up the political environment and speeding up the reaction times of politicians to issues and events. After 9/11, however, this phenomenon was reversed in the US with the Bush administration and its increased resistance to media pressure and the administration-managed coverage of the debate on the war in Iraq.

With respect to the new media and the Internet changing things, Iran again is a good example. If you wonder about the extent of things going on in Iran—because there is a clamp down on journalism—then new media has changed things. One could legitimately argue it is not the whole of Iran tweeting but at least it's a few strategically placed individuals who are sending footage of people being killed, of protests and so on and it becomes viral, etc. What this new media does is to give you a glimpse into a society that you may not have been able to see beforehand. It sheds light where there might not have been; however, whether or not it affects policy may be debatable. I don't think we are experiencing [the] same kind of effect like that of CNN in the past. What may be more of the case are campaigns not led by governments. This is changing. For example campaigns around Darfur and Bono's work, regardless of the value of these efforts, has increased awareness and debate on these issues.

Go digital, this is the future

Interview with Charles Warner, veteran media expert

T echnological innovations are happening at lightening speed, and with enormous impact on society. But the rise of new media has led to serious questions about the future of journalism. Will there still be newspapers in the future? If not, where will people get information? What are the new trends in media and journalism? What sort of ethical issues crop up in the new media era?

I asked all these questions to Charles Warner, a veteran media expert. Warner is an active blogger at MediaCurmudgeon.com, Huffington Post, and on Jack Myer's Media Biz Bloggers. He teaches media management, media sales, media economics, media ethics and competitive strategy at The New School and New York University in New York. In addition, he is a media management and sales consultant and trainer. He is the Goldenson Chair Emeritus at the University of Missouri School of Journalism, and a volunteer teaching assistant in the Family Program at the Metropolitan Museum of Art in New York.

Warner strongly believes that the media's future and (present) is online. "So I would give people advice, the same advice Columbia's School of Journalism gives its students; which is to go digital. Learn how to write HTML code. Learn to write great headlines for your blog post and go digital. That's where the expansion is, that's where it's going and you've got to be able to know how to do it and I think young people are generally good at that, so go digital!"

Could you give us some information about your background?

I started in the television business in 1957 and I worked in a television station in South Carolina, I was in sales. So I'd go out and I would sell an advertiser and then I would come home back the station and write the commercial and then we would shoot the commercial live. Then from television I got into radio. I worked in radio stations and I worked at CBS and

I was head of their radio sales division. Then I went to work for NBC ran some radio stations for NBC, but when I was with CBS and then later with NBC, one of the things I enjoyed the most about being vice president, general manager of the stations was, in those days CBS required all of its radio and TV stations to have a community affairs director and an editorial director. All of the CBS stations back in the '50s, '60s, and '70s had an editorial director and the general manager was required to do editorials on both radio and television. And if we think about what has happened since then, there are no TV stations, there are very few, that actually editorialize, and of course radio stations don't editorialize anymore either.

I got my Master's degree and then did my course work for my PhD. Then I taught at a small college in California and then went to the University of Missouri School of Journalism which is the oldest school of journalism in the US and then taught there for 10 years.

I wrote a textbook called *Broadcast and Cable selling* which I've updated, now it's called *Media Selling* and I've taught seminars on that book all over the world, including Russia, Georgia, and Poland. I have taught sales and advertising as a result of that book. Then I went from the University of Missouri School of Journalism to AOL. This was in 1998, so I was able to sort of be at the beginning of the internet. I retired and I teach at the New School and NYU.

Why is the University of Missouri: School of Journalism very important for journalism in America?

Well, it is the first school of journalism in America founded in 1908. And one of the things that the founding dean Walter Williams did at the time was to reach out to the world. It was one of the first openings that was made in China, and the University still has a very good association with China. It's been sort of a real universal school and so it's reached out universally. I've been to journalism schools in Poland, Russia, and Georgia sent by the school of journalism, to talk journalism with other countries. It was fascinating to see how different countries handle journalism and what journalism means. For the French it's all very theoretical and in some countries it's not and it's controlled by the government and that's interesting.

When the Missouri school was founded they had two departments—they had a newspaper department, they had a newspaper and they still do. The morning newspaper in Columbia, Missouri, is run by the journalism school. So they have a newspaper and they have an advertising department because they realized to have the news you have to support it somehow; so they taught advertising. And it was considered in educational circles, they called it the Missouri model because it's an undergraduate school plus a graduate school. So the undergraduates, [in] their freshmen and sophomore year take general courses and then you transfer to the journalism school and take undergraduate courses. And it's interesting because in academic circles there is sort of a great debate as to whether journalism should be taught at the undergrad level or only graduate. Many people say that you should get a broad education liberal arts education in your undergraduate and then go to Journalism school.

Columbia School of Journalism which was also founded in 1908 by Joseph Pulitzer but a bit later after the University of Missouri's, is a graduate school only. So Columbia people will say get a good liberal arts education and then get a professional education in journalism, the Missouri model is to do it at undergraduate level. It's very hands-on journalism because they own a television station and a newspaper. So the students actually go out and report at the television station, they are producers and reporters, they get hands on experience on television. They have professional anchors but other than that the students run it and it's the same with the newspaper. They have professional editors but the students actually get hands-on experience. Particularly these days and I see this as a right trend, that journalist should have a specialization in law or medicine or in economics.

What is its place in current trends in journalism?

I think there are several trends in journalism and the specialization is becoming more important; that is one of them. You have for example Paul Krugman who won the Nobel Prize, he's a journalist for *The New York Times* but he's also an economist. He is very powerful, very important. It's not just about politics anymore there are other areas too.

What about the other new trends in journalism, media and business?

Well since you asked, the Project for Excellence in Journalism (PEJ is a foundation and every year they do a survey for trends in journalism and in the one for 2009 six current trends are mentioned and I think they are very interesting.

Number one, they say there is a growing public debate on how to finance the news industry and that the news industry may be focusing on the wrong remedies while other areas go on unexplored. So I think that this is a huge debate, how are we going to finance journalism? With the focus often being *The New York Times*, sort of a journal of history as it were for America. What is going to happen to *The New York Times*? It has been terribly managed over a period of years and what's going to happen to it? It is a great newspaper, one of the greatest newspapers in America but has been mismanaged financially so is it going to survive? So they are really worried about whether it is going to be sustainable. Whether to charge or give it away? They borrowed $250 million from Carlos Slim, the Mexican financier, billionaire. So people are worried about whether he will take it over. People are worried about how to finance journalism.

They are looking at various models. The *Saint Petersburg Times* for example is one model. It's owned by the Poynter foundation. So should it be a foundation? Should it be a nonprofit like NPR? NPR has been very successful, WNYC here in NY [is] very successful. Clearly the best journalism in broadcasting is done by NPR and their stations and they are a foundation. We just went through a week, for those of you that listen, of their beg-a-thons, I gave our money and we do that twice a year, but that is where they get the majority of their funding. It is from contributions and that's a really good model because if you are involved and you pay your money, you are going to listen. It's sort of an involvement of the community and I think that that is really a very good model. Plus they get a lot of foundation money, NPR does, they got a huge grant from Susan Crock, Ray Crock's widow, who fought a big battle. I think she gave them 250 million dollars and that goes a long way when you think about the interest on that. So I think that there are a lot of ways to finance journalism and some that are not really being explored. I think there are much more creative ways to fund the *Times* and other journalistic enterprises.

The other thing that they said (the Project for Excellence in Journalism) and by the way if you just go on the web and go to their website "stateofthemedia.org" you'll see their complete report. It's really good because they do newspapers, radio, TV, and cable and they talk about all the various journalism outlets.

The second trend that they saw in 2009 was that power is shifting to the individual journalist, away by degrees from journalistic institutions. So what we see is, I've forgotten when it was, but recently they talked about what President Obama reads—there were jokes during when Bush was president that he never read anything, I'm sure it wasn't true, but you know, they said, "He doesn't read the *Times*, he doesn't read anything." But Obama is a terrific reader. So they published the things that he was reading. One thing that he reads every day is Andrew Sullivan's blog, The Daily Dish. So we see that writers like Paul Krugman and Andrew Sullivan—we can't possibly call them journalists. They're not even news reporters.

They're not journalists?

No. Somebody like Bill O'Reily, he's an entertainer. Rush Limbaugh, he is an entertainer. They're certainly not journalists. But they get much more attention and more focus on these personalities than on CBS News or NBC News. So I think that the focus is more on the individual journalist. And I think we'll see that, the star journalist, their blogs, and their books, what they report becomes more important often than the institution.

The third trend that they talked about was on the web, news organizations are focusing somewhat less on bringing news audiences in and more on pushing their content out. So what we see is that, for example, *The New York Times* is allowing Google—they don't block Google from going to *The New York Times*—so they get most of their traffic to *The New York Times* website through Google, from somewhere else. In other words, they're pushing their content out. So you go to the most popular blog, which is the *Huffington Post*, that just reached 40 million uniques, and it's very popular. And of course I know why people go there—it's to read my blog when I post it there. But it's become very popular. But what the *Huffington Post* is nothing but an aggregator.

Did any newspaper or news organizations sue them for aggregation?

No. I mean, it's a big issue. Rupert Murdoch is talking about putting code on its website so that they can't go from Google to the *Wall Street Journal*. But nobody is brave enough to do that, nobody has the courage to do that yet because they get so much traffic to all these news websites through Google. So what the news sites can do is to put code on their websites so that Google can't go there.

So, the next trend is the concept of partnership motivated in part by desperation in becoming a major focus of news investment and other prospects for the financial future of news. So these partnerships are with foundations, with sponsors, so we see on PBS, when you see Frontline or the News Hour with Jim Lehrer, you see Ford and various foundations doing sponsorships. And so I think we're seeing a lot of that now.

The next trend is really important; it's something to keep in mind. If cable news does not keep the audience gains of 2008, the rise of cable news is accelerating another change: the evaluation of the minute-by-minute judgment in political journalism. I mean, they're not doing any reporting anymore, they're just trying to be the latest to put up the latest scandal. And cable news particularly treats politics like a horse race. And all they talk about is strategy. I mean, they could hire sports reporters to go in and talk about it the same way they talk about the strategy of managing a baseball game. It's all about strategy, it's not about the issues, it's not about the ideas. They try to catch somebody in bed with somebody else. I mean, the biggest political story in 2008 was John Edwards' affair. So there's really no in-depth reporting on the issues whatsoever.

And then the last trend is, the press is more reactive and passive in its campaign coverage, and less of an enterprising investigator of the candidates than it once was. And I think again, this is a terrible trend. We're not doing the kind of investigative reporting that we should, that journalism was there for, the idea of bringing down the mighty. Mike Royko, the great columnist for the *Chicago Tribune*, a wonderful blue-collar guy, was terrific. He said that the relationship of a good reporter to a politician is the same relationship as a barking dog to a chicken thief. We don't see that anymore. We see just going along with whatever is happening. We're not investigating. And I know you're an investigative reporter and you've done that. It must be sad for you to see.

Do you think that there is a kind of self-censorship in the mainstream media because they rely on corporations?

Well, I don't think a lot of it; I think that if you look at television and cable news, I think that they're bland. They don't want to anger clients and the big sponsors, so they don't do a lot of investigative reporting on the economic issues. I think that they're careful about dissing the corporations that own them. There was a study years ago that was reported in the *Journalism Quarterly*, it was called "Social Control in the Newsroom." What it said was that editors don't tell reporters, "Don't write that," but the reporters know. They know what the culture in the newsroom is, and they know that they can't do this. It's just like when I was in Poland years ago, it was in 1992, and the television network in Poland was owned by the government. And you talk to the reporters, they know what they're not supposed to write about, and so they don't. It's sort of this social control. I think that's what we see, a sort of self-censorship.

Do you think that the absolute objectivity of journalism is impossible?

No. There is no such thing as objectivity. You just can't be objective. What you can be is fair and balanced. But the notion of objectivity is an economic notion not a journalistic notion. It was with the penny press back in the late 1800s where people said "wait a minute" because all newspapers used to be Catholic, Episcopalian, Tory, wig conservative or liberal, [be]cause that's what papers were, then somebody came up with the idea "if I can go right down the middle, I can sell twice as many newspapers." Like, ok let's be bland. Let's not anger anybody. Therefore we can sell twice as many newspapers or have as many listeners in radio or television. So objectivity is controlled by economics and not by any moral or ethical standards.

There is a very interesting discussion about Ethan Bronner,
The New York Times Jerusalem bureau chief, as you may know
his son was recently inducted into the Israeli army. What do
you think of this as a media critic?

Well, it's interesting there are people who will say that there is no way that a journalist reporting about Israel, when his son is in the Israel army, can be objective. And Bill Keller said he is a great reporter, he can be objective, it's fine. I think that the reason they defended it was economic as much as anything else. To have to take the guy out of Jerusalem, bring him back, take someone there, train the person. It would take 3 or 4 years to get the resources etc. So leave him there and if people want to complain about it, let them. I don't think that he can be objective but I don't think that matters because I don't think any reporter can be totally objective.

In one of your articles you claimed that advertisers should not cancel their advertising on Glen Becks' program. He had said that Obama is a racist on his program. There were some complaints and some organizations wanted the advertisers to stop sponsoring the show. You didn't agree. What's your argument?

So what I said was that under pressure from primarily a black orientated group, and they called themselves the Color of Change, they were calling up advertisers like Procter and Gamble, big advertisers, saying, "on Glen Beck's program on Fox News, he called Obama a racist. You should cancel your advertising." My point was that first of all, advertisers that cave into pressure, it's probably not a good idea to do that. They (the advertisers) are going on Glen Beck or Rachel Maddow, because they want to reach an audience and those personalities appeal to people and so they [are] supporting this idea of a public debate. But if they take them off because somebody protested them then that means they are giving in to pressure and I don't think that is a good idea. I believe, and what I wrote was if I were a P&G or major advertiser, I would take that as opportunity to come out with a press release and say that we do not agree with what Mr. Beck said, we think it was not a good remark, but we do defend to the death his right to say it. We agree with the notion that he can say it, so we are not cancelling our advertising.

How do you think new technologies will affect the future of media?

Yeah, it's just a matter of time. Newspapers can't possibly exist over a period of time by killing trees and printing. The blog "The Business Insider" that is edited by Henry Blodget had a chart. It was a blog post that said if *The New York Times* gave every one of its subscribers a Kindle, they would be ahead financially. That's how much it costs to print the paper; they've got printing presses bigger than this room. They've got dozens of them. They kill trees; the cost of distribution of that paper is huge. They've got union workers; they've got to pay off the mafia to distribute it. They've got all these expenses they'd be better off; they would be better off. Now books are a different thing, I don't know if the readers and the electronic delivery books will kill the book business but I think, maybe magazines definitely. It's just a matter of time; it has to be definitely.

What is the most important message you want to give young journalists just entering the profession?

I went to Saint John's University to give a lecture to students in the journalism department and there was a young student there who asked about television. And I said go somewhere else. If you want to be reporter on television or for a newspaper, forget about it. Because you are not going to make any money [with] newspapers and TV, they have been laying off people. Every week you hear stories. There were over a 105k jobs lost in the newspaper industry last year. That's a lot of jobs and the ones that are left, particularly out of the major markets, they don't make anything. The average salary of a TV reporter in a medium sized city? They don't pay them enough to live on. Why? Because the demand for the jobs is infinitely greater than the supply so they pay people nothing. So I would give people advice, the same advice Columbia's school of journalism gives its students, which is "to go digital." Learn how to write HTML code. Learn how to write great headlines for your blog post and go digital. That's where the expansion is, that's where it's going and you've got [to] be able to know how to do it and I think young people are generally good at that, so go digital!

The future of print media is at stake

Interview with David Rocks, Editor of Global News at Business Week

T he recent downturn in the economy has left virtually no industry untouched. Already in what some analyst proclaim to be a "death spiral," the print media industry in particular faces increasing pressure to justify its existing business structure.

Like nearly all magazines, *Business Week* has suffered from a decline in advertising during the late-2000s recession. Print revenues halved to US$60 million between 2006 and 2009, and online revenues only grew marginally to $20.5 million. In July 2009, it was reported that McGraw-Hill was trying to sell *Business Week* and had hired Evercore Partners to conduct the sale. Because of the magazine's liabilities it was suggested that it might change hands for the nominal price of $1 to an investor who was willing to incur losses turning the magazine around.

On October 13, 2009, Bloomberg L.P. announced it is acquiring the magazine for a reported $5 million, although exact figures were not disclosed. In a press release accompanying the announcement, Bloomberg chairman Peter Grauer said, "Together, the BusinessWeek.com and the Bloomberg.com websites have more unique visitors than any non-portal business and financial site." It is not known if Bloomberg plans any major changes to the magazine's design or editorial staff at this time. I have interviewed David Rocks, senior editor at Business Week, to discuss his magazine's future and contemporary issues in the news business.

So as we know there are claims that journalism is in a big crisis, and I just heard that Business Week was sold to Bloomberg. So could you please give us some information about this transaction, how did it happen and do you think that Bloomberg and its senior team are going to plan to make some changes in the editorial staff and the design of the magazine?

That's a lot of questions and there are a lot of answers, why did it happen, it's because Business Week has been losing money, a lot of money.

When did it start?

We've been in trouble, I'm not on the business side so I don't really know the details, but it's my understanding that we have either lost money every year or every year but one, since 2001; and we have seen our ad sales decline (that's where we get most of our money) every year or every but one since 2001.

There was a huge boom from 1998 to 2000, the E-business publication that I worked on which was our electronic business, The New Economy publication, was selling a 120 pages throughout the entire 1999-2000. In 2001, in our first edition we hoped to sell 32 pages, we scaled it back to 16, we scaled it back to 8 and then we killed it. So it was just off a cliff. So that's why we got sold.

And over the years—I'm not really privy to the numbers— but you will hear numbers in the $20 million year range of our losses, something had to give. McGraw hill, the company that owns us, they're looking to shore up their profits; they own Standard and Poor's which is also a company that is central to the economic crisis. They've seen their business fall off a cliff too, they wanted to do something that would [help] so they sold *Business Week*.

And although I think I was upset at the time, I have to say that I've come to the conclusion that it is really the best thing for *Business Week* at this time, I can't really envision a better outcome for us if you were to look at some of the other options, we were to be bought out by a Private Equity house. Their modus operandi is to strip and flip (what they call it in the business) which is to cut cost as much as possible, fire a whole bunch of people, and look for a buyer a couple years down the line.

Bloomberg has no intention of doing that, I don't think this magazine will ever be sold by Bloomberg. It might be shut down but it will never be sold. Do they plan changes? Unquestionably, after Steve Adler the editor-in-chief's leaving, they plan a redesign that they haven't really told us about, they are definitely going to be reassigning staffers from the magazine to Bloomberg news which has a very large organization, they've got 2400 journalist around the world, with us they'll have 2600, so I'm very optimistic about what is going to happen.

You have a very impressive bio, you actually studied philosophy. How did it happen, the jump to journalism, what made you decide to become a journalist?

On some level it was kind of accidental...

Do you think it was a mistake?

No, not a mistake, there are good and bad accidents and I will call this a good one. I had spent some time when I was in college in France and I loved it. I grew up in Colorado Springs which is a lovely but exceedingly provincial part of the United States. I couldn't envision going anywhere really. I had never been any where east of the Mississippi until I was 18 years old and so all of a sudden here I was in Paris and I thought wow and so I tried to figure out some kind of job that I could do that would allow me to live there or somewhere overseas. I always liked telling stories (been kind of a news junkie) and I just kind of fell into it, but it's been great.

You have worked many years in Europe, abroad, as a reporter, editor; I just want to know, how has it influenced your view of America?

Well, I suspect that any of you, anybody who has lived outside his or her home country for a period of time, it is an incredibly broadening experience and it makes you see the world through others' eyes. I think speaking English, for me speaking French, or Czech or any other languages that I speak, it's kind of like its living another life almost. There is the American me, and then there is the French speaking me who sees things [different] just by virtue of changing the language. When you are speaking [a foreign language] you start to see things differently and for me, living overseas, every day is an exploration, it's an adventure. Here to some extent you could say the same thing about New York, I'm not from New York but I have lived here for many years. I think it's also [the fact that] you're learning something, everything everyday, you're alive, you're a sponge taking in everything, that is why I like to live overseas. It has changed my perceptions of America I guess, broadened them.

Can you compare the journalism in Europe and the United States, in terms of the editorial process and in terms of the freedom of press?

I generally think that in terms of freedom of the press there probably isn't any place better than the US. I think that, but that is not to say that there is not a free press in virtually all of Western Europe and most of Eastern Europe now too, in fact. I think though it is a different kind of press. I think Europeans tend to practice what you might call advocacy journalism and I think that there is relatively little of that here [in the US]. I think there clearly are some cable news channels that are in a certain degree of advocacy, if you look at the *Washington Times* they make no secret about being very right wing. I think that in Europe, it tends to migrate more to the front page instead of the editorial page. So if you look at *Le Monde* in Paris, [it] is intellectual left, *Liberation* is the student left and *Le Figaro* is the business right and so papers have a certain ideological position that is not as well defined in the US. As much as some people might say that *The New York Times* is an instrument of the left, I honestly don't believe that is true of their news pages, they are very balanced, their editorial pages obviously have an advocacy position that leans towards the left; I think the *Wall Street Journal* has an advocacy position that leans to the right. But I think that their news pages really report the news very dispassionately.

What is the influence of the government in the US on media outlets?

Governments anywhere are going to have some level of influence, they make the laws, they try and spin things one way or another but I think that ultimately there is relatively little influence of government on the press in the US, certainly the White House has never called me up and said don't write that article, they didn't let me in once, but that was in the Regan White House.

Some governments banned some photography during the war times, didn't they?

Yes, the Bush White House did ban photography of the homecomings of the caskets of soldiers. They didn't actually ban publication if you managed to get the photographs; they just said you couldn't come to where you might be able get the photographs. And that's a nuance that I think is important, I wouldn't say I think that is good thing. And the Obama administration has in fact relaxed that, it feels like bad policy and overzealous spin, it doesn't feel to me like censorship or a lack of freedom of the press.

You're a senior editor of Business Week and from many countries your reporters send you photographs and stories, if they sent you photographs of severely injured American marines or soldiers would you run these photographs? Would you feel it unethical to publish or run these photographs?

The story of such a photograph... I can't imagine that story belonging in *Business Week* magazine. We don't cover politics in that way, but I wouldn't have an ethical or ideological reluctance to run it, I would just have a simple business reluctance to run it. Because it's not [a business story] you know we haven't had a reporter in Iraq for 5 years. We had somebody in there for 3 months in the beginning.

But you don't have anybody there?

No, we don't have anybody there; we don't have anybody in Afghanistan. We are a business magazine and our readers are interested in business around the world. On most levels there is not a lot of business in Iraq. I think that we could get some good stories out of there if we wanted to devote the resources but as I said we have been in a very resource-constrained environment. I fired somebody in Frankfurt, where there is clearly a lot of business; I'm not going to hire somebody in Iraq where there is a much more tenuous story for us.

Once we get going with Bloomberg, I actually hope to get some stories out of more far-flung places. That's really one of things that excites me most about cooperating with Bloomberg, they've got 145 bureaus in 70 something countries, 2200 journalist around the world and as foreign editor which is effectively what I am, that's a dream come true. I have a phone number of somebody in Kiev or in Ankara whom I can call and say "what's going on give me a story." They actually don't have anybody in Baghdad, they do have 1 or 2 people in Afghanistan and they've talked about being able to put somebody in Iraq. I'm hoping I will have access to those people to get more stories.

How do you think Bloomberg.com and Businessweek.com will contribute to each other?

That hasn't been decided and it's a decision that I personally will not have much input. Right now we have a deal with the Associated Press to provide us with a baseline of news, this is what's happening in such and such situation around the world with maybe 8 or 10 stories from AP on each page and then we've got our own stories as well. My suspicion is clearly that contract will be terminated and we'll go to Bloomberg for that, I don't know when, there may be some details in the contract which means will have to keep it for another couple of years or something. But at some point it's a no brainer that it has the Bloomberg copy.

It's my understanding though that Bloomberg recognizes that what they do is fairly substantively different from what we do, their target audience is people in finance and our target is more people in business and people who are interested in business. It's a nuance but I think that the kind of stories that we'll continue as Business Week will be more kind of corporate or management business oriented and the stuff that will come from Bloomberg will be more finance and market related.

How many reporters do you have abroad?

I have 13 correspondents who work for me now in Tokyo, Seoul, Hong Kong, Beijing, Delhi, Frankfurt, London, Moscow, Paris, and Mexico City.

What about Turkey?

No we don't. We have a magazine there called *Business Week Turkey*. But, that is not actually published by us, it's published under license by partners there, we have I think about 8 non-English language editions around the world, we've got China, Bulgaria, Thailand, and Indonesia etc. Turkish, I think is probably the best of the bunch, I think they do a very good job, I don't really read Turkish, so I can't really say, just from thumbing through it looks like a pretty good job and people who read Turkish tell me they do a really good job. Tell me if I'm wrong.

Yeah, you're right, and what do you think is the biggest challenge your reporters face in those countries as reporters?

The challenges change from place to place.

In China for example?

Asian cultures tend to be much more closed than American cultures. In America you'll call up a company and they will put the CEO on the phone, he'll start complaining about his dog and he will start telling you he went skiing or he skydives, they make really interesting stories, you can talk to them and they will tell you about themselves. There is a lot of kind of chest beating and macho behavior among American CEO's and that makes for fairly compelling stories. Asian CEO's tend to be much more self-effacing and Japan is actually worse than China in this respect. I don't know any detail about any Japanese executive, except that he golfs. So it's very difficult, and they don't speak, even when they are speaking in their native tongue they tend not to speak in interesting ways.

My job is to not only give you information but to give it to you in a way that you would actually want to read. And if you were reading most interviews with most Asian executives (there are a few exceptions) you'd fall asleep. So it's very difficult to coax stories out of these people. There are some exceptions; Masayoshi Son of Softbank in Japan, he's a great interview, and he's very outspoken who is willing to tell it like it is. In India, it's far less of a problem. In China, a lot of the private entrepreneurs tend to be very open or much more open than their Japanese counterparts. Chinese state-owned companies, forget it, everybody is absolutely terrified of saying anything that will get the ministry angry at them.

What do you think of Obama administration's efforts on fixing the economic crisis, the economic problems in the United States. Do you think that he's done well so far? Secondly, do you think he did enough for the peace process in the Middle East?

Those are obviously two very different questions and I'm not an economist, I'm not an expert on the economy nor am I an expert on the Middle East but in terms of whether the administration has done a good job with the economy, my sense is that they've done a pretty good job. Obviously economics, it's not chemistry, you can't dial back and say let's try this other thing. So there will always be a great amount of dispute as to whether they did too little, too much or just the right amount. People who are a lot smarter than me, whose opinions I tend to respect say that they did about the right amount. I feel like things are turning around, will they really turn around, I can't say, I feel cautiously optimistic about where we stand in the economic cycle right now. I feel cautiously optimistic, I feel cautiously confident, I should say that the Obama administration, did more or less the right thing. Could they have done something better? Absolutely. Do I know what it is? Absolutely not.

In terms of Middle East peace process, it's always a disappointment no matter who is in the White House. It never goes anywhere and it's distressing. Could they do more, no doubt, if they didn't have to try and deal with saving the global economy and reforming US healthcare, and everything else that they're doing. Is it enough, I wouldn't say it's enough but I wouldn't say it's not enough, it's hard for me to criticize for what they have done. Could they have done more? Unquestionably. Should something more be done? Absolutely. What exactly? You tell me.

Do you think it is fair to question the "Americanness" of the Muslims in the United States after events like Fort Hood shooting or September 11?

No, of course not. There is no way one should take the actions of one individual or 19 individuals and say everybody who is like that person is a terrorist or whatever else you want to say. So absolutely not, and that's what on September 11 they were doing. They were saying that everybody that lives in New York is an infidel and needs to be killed, so we would be stooping to their level if we did that, so of course not.

Understanding American
Islam in US media

Interview with Paul Barrett, author of American Islam

Paul Barrett set out to write a series of profiles of Muslim Americans that eventually turned into a book.

Former *Wall Street Journal* editor, Paul Barrett was working across the street from the World Trade Center on the day of the September 11 terrorist attacks.

In the year that followed, he edited the newspaper's front page, overseeing countless stories about Islam and its impact in far corners of the world, and realized that little was known about Muslims living in America. Americans tended to associate their Muslim neighbors with the violent and negative images of terrorists seen in news headlines. That's how he decided his research on Muslim Americans. His conclusion: There's a broad diversity of Muslims in this country, as diverse as the melting pot of America.

Barrett is now a writer and editor for *Business Week*. I interviewed him at the Turkish Cultural Center in New York, where he had been invited as a guest of honor for a luncheon program about his book *American Islam: The Struggle for the Soul of a Religion*.

How did you decide to write a book about Islam in America? What was your motivation?

When people first meet me, often the first question on their minds is "How did you come to write this book?" During that first year after 9/11, my primary assignment at *The Wall Street Journal* was editing stories for the front page. I spent most of that year editing stories about Islam in the context of other countries and other cultures. When my work-life returned to normal a year later, it occurred to me I knew more about

Islam overseas than I did in my own country. I found that incongruity strange. When I was able to get back into the swing of my own reporting, I decided to address it. I went out and gathered stories of individual people and individual communities in an effort to demonstrate the tremendous variety present in Islam in this country. And that's what this book is about: American Islam. In this country, many of the misunderstandings and misapprehensions we have about this religion stem from our confusion about who Muslims are and our tendency to merge and conflate the image of Islam and its adherents in the Middle East, Indonesia, Asia, Africa, Turkey, with the Muslims who may live across the street from us in New York, New Jersey, Connecticut, California. So one of the very first efforts I made was to demonstrate with these particular stories how American Islam is very distinct from Islam as it exists elsewhere. The main way in which it is distinct is that it is so varied. We basically have in this country the United Nations of Islam. We don't have one predominant group. We don't even have one group that dictates to others what Islam means in this country.

Most Americans think Muslims are of Arab descent. But most Arabs in the US are not Muslim. And most American Muslims are not Arab. Muslims are far better established and more integrated than most non-Muslims assume. Most private surveys show that Muslim family income is at the same level as non-Muslim Americans. The percentage of Muslims who have college degrees is just short of the general population. Even measures of civic participation, such as voter registration and intention to vote (60 to 70 percent) match the general population's rate. In my mind, that's fairly impressive when you understand the overall Muslim American population is two-thirds first-generation immigrants.

What was your approach?

In writing this book, my approach was neither that of a prosecutor nor a defense attorney. It is important to emphasize how mainstream Muslims, in my view, are an integration success story, though one sadly interrupted and disrupted by the fallout of 9/11. However, there is an undercurrent in this country of extremist ideological and religious thought, and it is one that concerns many Muslims, not to mention the government. There are extremist preachers in some mosques, and extremist literature. There are small groups who talk in a kind of apocalyptic, you know, "clash of civilizations" way about the inability of Muslim culture to integrate with the West. One of the great challenges that Muslims face is figuring out how to integrate people who are prone to this kind of thinking and how to diffuse that way of thinking. This is a real challenge and one I think Muslim organizations are coming to grips with as they take their responsibility to integrate their constituents into the larger society more seriously.

How did your subjects react when they learned of your Jewish background? How did you choose your seven subjects to follow and why did you not choose a Turkish subject, an Indonesian or a Bosnian?

I chose my subjects the way journalists tend to choose subjects: very unsystematically and serendipitously. You know, I started out with an imam who I'd met because his mosque is in Brooklyn. He happened to be African American, which in N.Y.C. represents a very substantial minority of Muslims. He also represents a story I thought my readers would already have some familiarity with: the story of the Nation of Islam and Malcolm X. What I wanted to show was that the roots of Islam in the African-American community do not begin with Malcolm X. It actually began in the 1600s and 1700s, with Muslim slaves brought to this country from West Africa.

Once I moved from the newspaper profiles to the book, I did try to broaden my selection to provide more examples to show diversity. But I did not burden myself with trying to find a representative of every subgroup. I knew it was going to be imperfect. I also felt there were certain elements that had to be represented: It seems to me you have to write about the very distinct Arab community of the American Midwest. I kind of had to address the issue Americans know the least about: white converts to Islam. I also wanted to address the issue of male-female Muslim relations, something Americans seemed to be fascinated by. I wanted to address the fact that many Muslims come to this country to attend a college or graduate school, which has been a major roadway for them to find their way into this country.

I was looking for surprising, interesting and illuminating aspects. If the book had 15 chapters perhaps I would have included a Turkish Muslim, etc.

I wrote a piece for the *Los Angeles Times* about the book. As I recall, the headline read, "Writing about Muslims while Jewish." What I said in that article was that while my being Jewish at times did provoke a certain amount of skepticism and concern, over the long term it actually was a tremendous advantage. It was a kind of icebreaker to essentially explain to a skeptical group of interview subjects as they auditioned me why they should tell me anything in detail. And frankly, I auditioned them, too. My method was to try and focus in very tightly on individuals and families, and to be able to do that you need to be able to pick from the crowd people who are willing to tell their story candidly, and not speak in press releases and speeches and tell their story in human terms.

As for Asra Nomani, one of the characters you profile, to what extent does she represent Muslim women in America?

First we have to back up and explain who Asra Nomani is. Asra is an Indian immigrant who came here as a very young child. Her family story is very common in American Muslims' stories. They came here because her father was a graduate student at West Virginia University. He came to this country to get an education and ended up settling in Morgantown, West Virginia. He became a professor, a prominent citizen in town and an elder in the Muslim community. He was one of the founders of the mosque in Morgantown.

Now the story that I wrote about Asra in some ways begins with the opening of the new mosque in Morgantown. One of the interesting aspects of the mosque's design is that it was built with a women's prayer balcony. In the old mosque, the women prayed behind the men. In the new mosque, women were relegated to a separate balcony with a wall preventing them from seeing over. This event in and of itself was remarkable: It's always interesting to see how a religious group that has transported itself to a new culture makes what seems like a counter-intuitive move back towards orthodoxy. But in fact it's quite typical among religious immigrant groups in this country for a second generation to become somewhat more orthodox than the first generation, which is more oriented toward establishing itself and playing down its religious orientation. Historically you can see this in second generations of Jewish and Catholic immigrants.

But here is this new arrangement, and Asra, who had grown up as an American and considered herself a feminist, though an observant Muslim, felt very alienated and frustrated by this arrangement. She thought it was almost sacrilegious the way she was cut off from the imam and couldn't see what was going on.

And she announced she was simply not going to follow those rules. She was going to pray in the back of the main prayer hall, as was done in most countries throughout the world. She began praying in the back of the prayer hall. She had her niece and her mother with her. They weren't doing anything loud or brash. But this led to a big blow-up in the community. She was chastised by male members of the congregation. Her father was ostracized; he was one of the founders of the mosque, and he was basically driven out of his leadership position by men he had known for 25 to 30 years. And soon her experience there and the controversy had emanated out to other congregations around the US, where her story was very meaningful to a lot of other Muslim women of her generation who shared some of her frustrations. So that's why I chose to tell her story. The tension reflected in her life, her effort to bridge East and West, tradition and modernity, I think are very prevalent in the lives of many women even if they don't go to this end.

Do you think that Muslim voices are not represented in the mainstream media?

I think 10 years ago that assumption could be correct, but today that is less accurate. If you and I wanted to sit down at a computer and go through a media database, we would find quite a few articles describing Muslim life in the US, including articles that reflect Muslim political views as well as op-eds. In the digital world there is no shortage of Muslim voices, but how many people are going and virtually sitting in an audience and listening to those Muslim voices? There are many very sophisticated Muslim websites.

Earlier, you mentioned that the Muslim college graduation rate is somewhat less than that of the general American population. Can you explain this?

My point actually was how striking it is to me that the rates are very similar. Muslims are more integrated and more successful than many

Americans understand. A very substantial fraction of Muslim immigrants come to this country for higher education. That's why they've been so successful; they don't come here and start on the lower rungs.

Some short-term developments that we have alluded to are very interesting: People now in college, in their 20s and 30s, are reverting to tradition. They have parents who came here and identified themselves primarily through their nation of origin, and thought of themselves as Egyptians, Lebanese, Indian, not as Muslims. But their children, who grow up speaking with American accents and going to American schools, find themselves living with one foot in a traditional environment and one foot in an American world, and it's quite common that when they go off to college, pertaining to socializing, dating, alcohol, they find a different environment. And their reaction is to re-embrace religion as a form of identity, something they can meet other people through and gain a sense of solidarity. So you have this fascinating phenomenon where people in their 20s might dress in a conservative way while their parents might have a more secular appearance. It's not unusual for Muslim student associations on campuses to be fairly orthodox in their practices. My guess is that over time this will become part of the longer history of second generations re-embracing tradition, as opposed to being a permanent development.

One last thought: You shouldn't discount the effect of 9/11, which served as a catalyzing event in all senses of the word, good and bad. It stirred suspicion and bigotry at certain levels. It also sparked greater communication along religious and ethnic lines. In my experience, despite the trauma and despite the FBI investigations and despite the nasty words that may have been exchanged on the street during the trauma of 9/11, many Muslims, particularly immigrants, who want to stay, are going to bring the foot that was still in the old country and plant it here. That doesn't mean that they're going to become "Wonder bread, apple pie" Americans overnight, but that they're demanding to be Americans. It's a very complicated process, not necessarily a linear development, as Professor Herbert taught us about Catholics and Jews.

Muslims and Christians can learn from *The Saint and the Sultan*

Interview with Paul Moses, Pulitzer Award winner journalist

The shooting at Fort Hood in Texas have sparked a renewed interest into the roles that Muslims play in American society. Tensions that were once at an all time high after the events of September 11, for some, seem to have again been ratcheted up after this recent tragedy.

It is within this context that I sat down with Paul Moses, professor of journalism at Brooklyn College, to discuss his new book, *The Saint and the Sultan*, a book written in part as a reflection on the tensions between Muslims and Christians after the events of September 11.

Moses is a former senior religion writer, City Hall bureau chief and city editor at *Newsday*, where he was the lead writer in news coverage that won a Pulitzer Prize.

I think his book *The Saint and the Sultan* is a very important and timely book. The book reminds us that the true believers of dialogue and constructive encounters must be courageous enough to talk as well as to listen, even opposing their own people, in the name of justice, dignity and love.

Mr. Moses, can you please tell us how you happened to write this specific story? How did it come about?

I just came upon it in my reading. There was this little book about St. Francis that goes back to the 1300s called *The Little Flowers of St. Francis*, a collection of stories about St. Francis, some of them true, some of them legendary. I saw this, and it was in this period some time after September 11. There was so much tension between Christians and Muslims here in New York and elsewhere, and here I was reading this story about

St. Francis meeting the sultan during the middle of the Fifth Crusade. They are getting along, and I thought, "Wow, this is great; could this possibly be true?" I began to research, and it was well documented from sources in the thirteenth century. It just intrigued me and seemed like it would be worth telling in more depth.

Give us more details about this saint. Why do you think he was different from the other saints? And why do you think that he was so famous?

He really stands out for Christians amongst all the saints, and I call him the most beloved saint since the time of the apostles. There is just something about him that even in his lifetime towards the end of his life people already knew he was holy and was to be named a saint through the process that the Church had. He just gave so totally of himself to other people. He was so gentle, and so it is hard to explain why him. There are many other great saints, of course, but just for some reason from early on, he had a special place in the hearts of Christians. It's hard to answer, really, but I guess because of his great goodness, holiness and generosity of spirit not only to people, but to animals and nature. There is something about him that even today, people really like him. Even people who are not really religious themselves.

What I knew about him was that he liked animals, but in your book he looks like a controversial figure. Do you agree with that?

Yes, I think that is true. Yes, we have this image of St. Francis today as this patron saint of animals. When we see a statue of him, it's usually with a bird on his shoulder or in his hands, and I think that's true. He did have a special affection for animals, but I also see him in a much different way. If you really look closely at his story, first of all what he did in his own time was shocking to people. He refused to have any possessions, and he dressed in a way that was shocking to people that made a statement to other people that he was living a simple, pure life, that the other people were too attached to their material things. So right away it's hard for us to imagine such a thing because we have such a sense of St. Francis as very peaceful and peace-loving figure, which he was, but just by what he did, the example he set, to the people around, he was controversial. He was actually subject to a lot of abuse when he changed his life to live in a simple way. People would throw things at him, and people would beat him up. His friars, as he began to send them out through Europe, were attacked frequently. They were at risk of being accused of heresy, and even worse things happening to them, and so, we don't think of Francis as being a controversial figure. But he was.

In one of your interviews, you say that we have to look very closely at why he changed his life. Can you explain this?

Well, I portrayed his journey to the Sultan during the crusade as a mission of peace, and I think to understand that we have to understand what made St. Francis change his life. When St. Francis grew up, he was the son of the richest merchant in his town of Assisi. There was constant violence in central Italy at that time; Assisi was going to war with its larger and more powerful neighbor, Perugia. So Francis was a soldier in that war as a knight. He was on horseback, and they went off into battle. The Assisians were massacred, and Francis saw that. People he knew were all being hunted down like animals and killed. Francis survived because he was taken prisoner. Being the son of a very wealthy man, the Perugians knew they could get a good ransom for him, and so he was taken and thrown into a deep hole in the ground where he lived for a year. It was very damp and had very little light, and he was chained. That experience shattered him psychologically and to an extent physically also, so Francis, after he was finally released, was a hollow man. He began to recover probably through prayer and contemplation, and that started the process. If you know the story of Francis, you know the steps to it, but that started the process, where he separated himself from the things of his time. He renounced his old identity, renounced all his belongings. He even had to separate himself from his family because his father was so angry at him and established this new identity as someone who was going to live a very simple life of penance. So when we look at Francis, when he went on the Fifth Crusade, we have to remember that he is somebody who knew about warfare. It really bothered him. What he saw going on in Egypt during the Crusade really bothered him. He wanted to find some other way. He was loyal to his faith, and he was loyal to the Pope. But he didn't like what was happening.

*The main reason for Francis to go to the Sultan and to talk to him
was actually to convert the Sultan, is that correct?*

That's right. Francis hoped to convert the Sultan and thereby end the
crusade.

Yes, but did it work?

It didn't work. The Sultan was a good Muslim, and he believed in his
faith. I think if we look at him, it shapes his actions, throughout the war
and in his dealings with Francis. I guess that it is a controversial thing
today that he was trying to convert him, but I talked to different Muslim
scholars about that, and their feeling was that Francis was doing this differently from the way it was done in his time. First of all, he went to the
Sultan totally unarmed, and there was no hint of coercion on his part. He
said to the Sultan, "If you wish to speak to me, I will tell you so." It was
an offer the Sultan could have refused. So I think what was important
about going to the Sultan was the spirit of peace that he went with.

So can you please detail what exactly they talked about?

Yes, well the records aren't clear enough to know for sure exactly what
they spoke about. One difficult thing in writing the book was that in that
period of history they weren't writing letters much or things like that, so
there is not that detail. But what we do know is that Francis would have
greeted the Sultan, and the sultan allowed him to speak and even to
preach in his camp for like three days. We know that the Sultan had his
own religious experts there, and I would say Francis would have probably approached the Sultan on some common ground because if he had
said things that the Sultan's religious experts would have said to him
that he couldn't have this conversation, if Francis had, for example, criticized Muhammad, if he had criticized God in some way, I think the conversation would have ended. It wouldn't have gone on for three days. So
I think in Francis we get those insights into the conversation, but I
couldn't give you a dialogue without making it up.

*Can you please tell us about Christians' perceptions of Muslims and
vice versa during that time? And how do you think that the Christians
or Francis were changed after these meetings with the Sultan?*

I think in terms of perceptions, there are two levels here. One is that
Christians and Muslims did business with each other, they traded. There

were Christians that came from Venice and Genoa. They were in Egypt and doing business, quite a few, and the sultan encouraged that kind of trade. Then second, there is what I guess is really a wartime propaganda. So the Christians portrayed the Muslims, especially their leaders, in a kind of animal like/animalistic kind of imagery. So Francis would have not known much about Muslims when he was going there. Probably he thought what he was doing as extremely dangerous, which it was. It was wartime. He had crossed over into the enemy's camp unarmed, and so it was dangerous.

The Sultan is a little different because he had more experience in dealing with Christians than the Crusader army or Francis would have, because Egypt has a Christian population. So the Sultan had extensive dealings with the Coptic Christians in Egypt and was perhaps in all of Egypt's history probably the closest to the Christians of Egypt. He was often called on to mediate their disputes. For example, there was a big dispute over who would be the Coptic patriarch of Egypt, and the sultan always did this with great sensitivity for the religious traditions of the Christians. He didn't impose his own person there or anything like that. So there is a book called *The History of the Patriarchs of Egypt*. It's a medieval account of the Egyptian church, and it creates a very favorable portrait of Sultan Melek-el-Kamel.

Were you inspired to write this book because of the horrible effects of September 11? Can this be inferred?

That certainly had something to do with it. It made this story timely. I wrote about September 11 when I worked for *Newsday*. At the time, I wrote the main story, and it was my job to take all these terrible things people saw and felt and combine them into one news story. I had been a religion reporter at *Newsday*, and so I was thinking a lot in terms of how could religion be the basis for this. What is "real" religion? What is authentic about religion? And when is it being used falsely? So I was thinking a lot about that, and I think that both Francis and the sultan give us the real authentic religion that they are from. So Francis really wanted to return Christians to their early traditions of the time of the apostles.

Francis reminds Christians that their religion is rooted in nonviolence, which by the time of the Crusades had definitely been lost. And the Sultan brings up an interesting Muslim tradition, too, which is

respect for holy Christians, especially holy Christian monks. It's a tradition that goes back to the earliest days of Islam; the Prophet Muhammad
would have known Christian monks in the desert. There are a number of
experts on Islam who pointed this out to me. One who stands out in my
mind right now is Mahmoud Ayoub, who is now at Hartford Seminary.
He was a professor at Temple University when I spoke to him; he felt
that this is important for Muslims to focus on, this tradition in Islam. So I
said Francis points Christians to their tradition; the love of enemies is a
part of tradition often forgotten. So they both do that, I think. You know,
it's distressing to see religion used for evil, and so both of them point out
us to what's good in their traditions. That's one of the things that
appealed to me in the story.

**You portrayed Islam and the Sultan in a very positive way in
your book. Were you criticized for that?**

I have not been. I was afraid that I might be because, you know, sometimes I write online on blogs and so forth, and the blog world can be
very crude. I was wondering. But that hasn't happened, and I am glad.
However, it was something that I was aware of as a possibility. In fact,
the reviews that I am seeing have all commented on the portrait of the
Sultan in a positive way, but you know, I didn't start out that way. As a
journalist, my sense of someone who is in charge of the country, you
know us journalists, we tend to be suspicious of people in authority, but
it was only as I really researched more thoroughly, got to know the Sultan as a man, I really saw him as a special person. He ruled Egypt for 40
years, 20 years as viceroy, and 20 years as Sultan. And he did it really
well, and as I said, I think his religious views shaped him. He was also
very practical. He knew that the best thing to do was to avoid war if you
can, for practical reasons. So his inclination was always to try to encourage trade with the enemy and encourage negotiation if there was war.

At the end of the Crusades, Christians had managed to get ways into
Egypt. They conquered Damietta, which is at the mouth of the Nile, and
then they went further. They didn't really know where they were going,
and the Sultan's soldiers were able to raise the level of the Nile and
trapped the Christian soldiers. So they could have killed every one of
them, but that would have served no good purpose at the time, and it
would have only incited further warfare. So the Sultan shocked them by

feeding the Christian army and providing them with safe passage out of Egypt, and at the end, they praised him. The leader of the expedition is this kind of person. He wrote to the Sultan and said truly that he was Kamel, meaning perfect, right? and so it ended on that note. I think the Sultan is an important historical figure, also. You know St. Francis is so famous, so I try to make the sultan an equal partner in the book.

What do you think Muslims and Christians can learn from your book when we look at the issue in terms of the political tensions between them?

Yes, in terms of religion, there are some good things going on right now. There is the Common Word initiative. I think things like that are a good start. I guess one thing is to not demonize others that you don't know. I think that is another thing that I have learned from looking closely at Francis. All around him people demonized the enemy, and Francis never says (in all the writings) anything negative about all the Muslims. I'm sure in his mind they were missing out on salvation, but he never says anything negative. You never hear "infidel" or anything like that. I think that it is important for us on both sides: How we approach the other and yes, we don't share the same beliefs, but we are people. And I think that is part of the example mentioned above.

Maintaining balance in turbulent times

Interview with Greg Winter, Editor of The Foreign
Desk at The New York Times:

G reg Fabian Winter is a Foreign Desk Editor at *The New York Times*, responsible for Latin America and Africa coverage. He previously worked as a reporter, covering education and business. In the following interview, Winter discusses the challenges of providing foreign news coverage in these pressing times, when newspapers are cutting back budgets and the internet is replacing traditional mainstream media. A staunch believer in the power of truth telling, Winter says "*The Times* will continue to stick to its mission of delivering global news, at a time when the public may prefer celebrity gossip soundbites."

Winter takes us through the inside process of deciding the daily news and shares his insights on reporting such events as the Israel-Palestinian conflict.

How long have you been working as a journalist and
how and when did you decide to be a journalist?

I actually have an untraditional, unorthodox path into journalism. I worked as a homeless advocate and public policy director in San Francisco after college for a number of years building houses for homeless families and trying to develop a coordinated strategy for the city of San Francisco in terms of dealing with issues of poverty, substance abuse, homelessness, welfare, things of that nature and I decided that I was tired of smashing my head against a very solid brick wall. It was not moving at all. So I am very interested in writing and obviously interested in social issues so I transitioned to journalism about 10 years ago and what I did not expect actually is how much you can actually change things and move the ball within journalism. I was not always working as a foreign editor, I was a writer for five years of *The Times* and I wrote about education, business and national news. You know one story can spark legislation in congress and really change the major issues. It teaches you to be very careful about what you say and teaches you to be very, attentive to details, what you write because people really watch them.

How many correspondents do you have all over the world right now?

Right now probably in the order of 40 correspondents working around the world in various bureaus and then those correspondents work also with a number of stringers, so for example, any given country (for example my area that I supervise is Latin America, Africa and UN) but we all have to dabble pretty much in everything because they are not enough of us in terms of editors. And one of my correspondents, for example, is based in Nairobi and he covers all of East Africa. It is impossible for one person to be in upwards of 20 countries at any given time, so he has a network of journalists that he works with who we pay locally in places like Somali, Uganda, Rwanda, Congo—all over the place, who can feed him information when things are developing so that he can know what is occurring around the region.

Do you think the quality for the coverage has been impacted by the recent cutbacks in the news industry?

Generally, around the country with regard to American media there has been major closure of bureaus around the world. For example just look at Iraq, if you are talking about the time of invasion you probably have upwards of 100 organizations that have permanent presence or some kind of continuing presence in Iraq. Now you have about five news agencies in the US that have a permanent presence in Iraq. The *Times*, like any news paper, has had major financial constraints everybody probably read about, it has not yet impacted foreign coverage. There has been a very concerted effort on the part of the paper to maintain foreign bureaus not cut them back, sometimes we trade one bureau for another. So for example we closed one in Jakarta but we are going to open additional slots in India for example. We may do some of that trading but we haven't reduced the number of overall correspondents. I hope that doesn't change. It is still very expensive to cover foreign news. Our bureau in Bagdad for example costs more than three million dollars a year. It costs a hundred Iraqi journalists, as well as security guards, as well as translators who we hire, so these things are extremely expensive to maintain that is why there is a lot of pressure on Wall Street, especially for public companies, to reduce your spending on news gathering. Locally at the *Times* we have a strange stock situation where the publisher, the family actually owns the controlling stock so while Wall Street always is calling on us to severely cut the newsroom the family resists. So I hope that maintains a balance quite a while.

When you send correspondents throughout the world, how important is it that they speak the local language and have some in-depth knowledge of the region they are covering?

It depends. Obviously it is always important, as far as language training it depends on where they are going. If they are going to China for example we typically put the correspondent in language training for a year before they go. Some people who are going to China have been experts in China for a long time, they speak Chinese before they sign up for the post. If you are going to Paris there are people who speak French already. We don't have to put them into language training, probably just insist on someone who knows French before hiring. So it depends on where you are going. But generally there is always primacy on the correspondent speaking a language but that doesn't mean that they won't rely on translators as well. Often times a correspondent will learn to be able to conduct all of their interviews in the local language within a relatively short time being there. Let's say, after the first year and then they have a few more years where they can pretty much go on their own.

How do you go about covering a story like Israel-Palestine situation for example? And how do you maintain balance in covering something that is this sensitive?

Well, in truth nobody is happy with the coverage of the Middle East. And sometimes that is a major sign that you are doing a good job because you are heading extremely angry responses from readers who are favoring the Palestinians and from readers who favor Israelis. Amazingly there is a balance in terms of angry response of them. And they are extremely vociferous. Personally I would hate to be the Jerusalem bureau chief. That is a very tough job. The strategy for covering something like Gaza is multiple, manifold. First of all, you have the problem of not getting into Gaza yourself. So that is a very difficult problem, luckily the *Times* has a correspondent who is Palestinian and who lives in Gaza. We had somebody there from day one. In fact, the moment the air strikes started, people were fleeing away from the buildings, she ran toward them. She has been there for a long time. She covered the Second Intifada, she covered the battle between Hamas and Fatah, so she started going straight toward the missiles, straight toward the hospital and she was there throughout the entire time and she wrote a number of front page stories from there. Now, she was very endangered by her coverage. First of all, she lived in Gaza in an apartment building. She lived near various important sites that were constantly being bombed. She had a very difficult time of sleeping at night. She slept with the windows open since the bombs could shatter the glass. She slept under a table because of air strikes. In a situation like that I may know my neighbors a little bit but I don't know who lives in the apartment down the way. I don't know if that person is wanted by Israel or suspected by Israel to be some kind of a militant. I don't know the family next door, maybe they are nice but I don't know what the status of their son [is]. There is constant fear when she is reporting and she is going around to the various areas alone. She could not obviously do it alone. Later as the conflict started to wane we were actually able to also get Sabrina Tavernise who is the Istanbul bureau chief. She was able to come and she was a very experienced war correspondent, she covered the Hezbollah War, she was in Iraq for a long time so she is very good in those situations but in addition to that we had two of our Jerusalem correspondents who were writing every day. We also had our Paris correspondent who used to be the Jerusalem bureau chief; he was going to the border of Gaza through Rafah after Egypt. Now how do you make sure that everything is fair? Now, first of all, any journalist has to apply the measures of fair journalism. You know, this really angers a lot of readers. Because Israel would say things and reporters would report it. Reporters might offer evidence or an assertion. Let's take a specific example, the shelling of the UN school. Outside of the school, innocent people were killed. Israel says fire was coming outside of the school, they were responding to the fire and other types of militants there. So the story will include the assertion by Israel. The story will also include the assertion by the UN, saying "look, that is not true, we had no knowledge of any activity in the area. We have no reason to believe there are any militants there." The story also found somebody who was in the area, "yes, I think, there was somebody who is known to be militant, but he was several hundred yards away..." These are all things that you do as a journalist. You try to report what each side says as well as you try [to] find whatever independent confirmation you can. But all three of those things anger the readers depending upon where you are coming from. You will hear one side that says the UN, especially INRA (the organization working in Gaza), historically has a bias so anything they say will be against Israel. You cannot possibly include anything they said. The problem you have as a journalist is that by doing your job you will be open to very vociferous criticism on both sides. The only thing you can really do is to try to be consistent in what you do. You do a story about Palestinians mourning the deaths of many civilians in Gaza. We did several of those and you make sure that at some point you are also doing a story about Israelis' mourning deaths, when they occur as well. The question then becomes should you do more stories on the Palestinians' dying than you do on Israelis' dying. Of course you end up doing it that way because news drives in that way but many pro-Palestinian readers would say "Why would you even include any stories on Israelis' dying when they were such a small proportion of those who die?" It is a very difficult balance in the end. It includes not only the articles that you write, because each day you might have four or five articles on the conflict itself, you try to include the right mix each day as well as the right mix of pictures as well as the right mix of headlines, but whatever you do you are going to be criticized very angrily. That is fine, that is part of democracy. I am not saying that you should not be criticized.

What kinds of measures do you take to guarantee the safety of your correspondents in these kinds of conflict regions?
Well, we give them flak jackets and helmets and body armor in Iraq; we provide them with armored cars secured with bodyguards.

Do they have bodyguards?
Yes, sure. Lots of bodyguards. It used to be that you could go into Gaza when things were getting very heavy, they sometimes would go around with a team of bodyguards. In some places you can't operate without

that. Three million dollars spent, a lot of it is for security. It is over a hundred people strong, the Iraqi staff and about a quarter of Iraqi journalists and translators but there are a lot of bodyguards, drivers, translators, security consultants. Ultimately however, if you are in a war, if you are going to a country like Zimbabwe, where many reporters often go, there is always so much you can do. I have many reporters arrested and held, sometimes by the government, sometimes by separate agents who have a political ax to grind. We had reporters held by the Taliban in Afghanistan. In the end, it is the choice of the reporter whether they want to go. We do not force a reporter to go into that type of situation in which their life is going to be in danger. That is their choice. It turns out that most reporters who are foreign correspondents are motivated by an intense interest and desire to get the story. So we often times have to hold them back. I say maybe this is not the best time to go into Zimbabwe, given they have arrested reporters. Have you considered the security measures that you have to take? But it is very difficult to be the boss of somebody who is deciding to go risk their life. And people do get killed, we actually had two Iraqi correspondents killed in the past seven years. Sometimes just working for a news agency makes you a target. We had one person just recently killed in Bagdad who was clearly assassinated and the only reason was he worked for *The New York Times*.

Can you give some details about the process of putting a story in the paper? For example, how do you decide which foreign photos land on the front page?

We actually don't decide which foreign photos land on the front page. Front page is its own entity, if you will. The front page web site is a separate entity. But I will talk about the paper. There are obviously multiple sections in *The New York Times*. There is foreign news, which is obviously a very critical one. There is business and these days business is very important, obviously. There is national news, there is metro. There is sports. There is culture. There is dining. There are a million different sections. Some of them are never going to be in the front page. But everyday all of main news sections go to a meeting twice a day with the top editors of the paper, including the executive editor, the managing editors and the people who decide [to] hear pitches from us, just like our reporters pitch stories to us and say I want to do this and we say that sounds good or I don't know I would skip that [and] focus on something else. The heads of each of these news sections go to the front page and say "yesterday we had multiple foreign stories that we think you should consider." We once had the story about an investigation. There was a story about Hamad Karzai's brother, the entrepreneur. There were further stories about the attacks on the cricket team in Pakistan. There was the international criminal court issue for President Basir of Sudan. These are a number of stories and these are foreign stories. So the front page editors have to decide which of all those they are going to put on the front page. We don't control that, we try to influence it best we can. But in the end the decision is not ours. The same thing is for the photo. Photo editors go and show the pictures. Sometimes it is a compromise. For example in today's paper you notice that the picture of president of Sudan is on the front page but the article is inside the paper. You get half of what you are looking for. So we don't really control the front page. As far as the inside foreign section, however, we can have more control over that, there is a separate picture editor but she will show us in the course of the day the kinds of pictures that she is looking at various stories. If we have a problem with one of the pictures because it does not match the story then we would say so. That becomes particularly important in issues, like you are saying, covering the Gaza war because we have a ton of pictures of dead Palestinians which we did and ran everyday. Then we might also say ok well in the next day let's make sure we have a picture of [a] funeral in Israel from a rocket attack. Again, it is a judgment—there is no science to it. It is all a judgment call.

So we can say that The New York Times isn't just influential in the US but all over the world. When The New York Times gives a certain story attention, the world will pay attention.
We would like to think so but I don't know...

I am curious if American readers are really interested in what is happening in Sudan?
A lot of the stories that we put on the front page are not things that American readers necessarily are interested in. And we are aware of that.

What is the reason?

Because the people don't necessarily want to take their medicine either but you have to give it to them just because Americans might be more interested in Britney Spears than in Omar Bashir. That does not mean we are going to change our approach to covering, what we think are the most important stories of the day. If you would govern by that then we would be a very different newspaper. There is some attention to try to get what we might call a light story on the front page. Obviously the front page is dominated by bad news most days, a lot of [our] news is dominated by bad news. So the front page is conscious of trying to get some kind of light feature, sometimes on the front page something that maybe a little bit more entertaining than just sad but that only sort of reinforces the notion that their primary job is to designate what we think that the most important stories of the day, the most important occurrences, and to signal that to the readers.

Can we say that The New York Times is an "agenda setter" of the world?

It depends. I think that honestly the hegemony of the mainstream press has definitely lessened in recent years. My own personal theory (this is not the theory of *The New York Times*) is that while the proliferation of news outlets on the internet has been beneficial in many ways, it actually detracts from people's understanding of what is going on in the world. There was a time period in which you had a great powerful mainstream press and as a result you had a greater common understanding and focus of what's going on in the world. Now I am not saying that the picture of the world was always accurate or always perfect, but you did have a greater solidification or common set of understanding in principles of what was happening in the world. Currently what you have is if you are a believer of a right wing agenda or if you have right wing sympathies you have no reason to pay attention to what is necessarily in the mainstream press. You can go straightly to FOX news. And your view of the world will be entirely shaped according to your personal political preferences. So the same goes on the left; you could read a blog or you could read a particular outlet that is suited to your own ideological preferences. As a result, the two readers that we are talking about have wildly different conceptions on what is going on in the world; what is actually happening is that people are operating not only from different political perspectives but from a wildly different set of facts. And I don't actually think that that is necessarily a great service to public debate. You have a very scattered conception on what is actually happening in this country and in this world. And it does not necessarily serve political discourse because people end up being unable to talk to each other about the same issue.

Do you sometimes question the reliability of the stories sent to you from your correspondents, and what kind of measures do you have for the accuracy of the stories?

You have to challenge if any time a correspondent is making an assertion in a story. First of all, if they are making an assertion in the story as a matter of a fact, as an assertion of fact, if it is not understood to be a mutually accepted fact, it needs to have attribution, it needs to have a source. You have to say "where did you get that fact, is it coming from this particular government or agency?" That is basic journalism; it has to have attribution. If you feel like the reporter is making an assertion, for example, of a trend that is occurring or some other assertion that is not merely a fact, but an assessment. There are issues of fact and then there is "how did you bring these facts together" to say what is the story that we're actually telling provides some analysis on what is going on. If the person is making an analysis you don't think that is substantiated by the fact. Then that is your job as an editor to make sure that any assertion or analysis is going to be substantiated by fact. That should be spelled out in the story more or less. Not every single attribution is going to be listed in the story because there is something we may have reported multiple times that we may know already to be the fact. But for the most part everything should be well substantiated. As far as the agendas, your question is also asking "is somebody pushing a particular personal agenda?" I think that most of the reporters you know over time and you know sort of what they think about "x" and "y," so you are able to police them. You are able to say "ok, I know you don't like this person very much because you think that he is bad guy. But really you don't need to call them a dictator; you can call them an authoritarian president. I think everybody would agree. So there are some ways of policing people over time, just because they are human beings and they have natural preferences. Mostly I don't really feel like there are strong agendas on the part of the correspondents. Correspondent never let their personal biases get in the way of a good story. For example, I was an education writer for a long time as well as a business writer. I am personally in favor of affirmative action. In terms of an educational policy I probably should not be saying that but I am saying "I believe that affirmative action has been an important tool to rectify educational discrimination over the years." But as an educational writer I certainly had to write stories in which new social science findings came out saying that affirmative action did not work for one reason or another or there is a new research study coming out debunking the affirmative action for this or another. So as a journalist you don't let your personal feelings get in the way of a story. That is why you are there, you are there to be the deliverer of the information and to provide an analysis. So the correspondents are seasoned journalists. They are not there because they are pushing an agenda.

I remember the story of your Istanbul bureau chief about the Turkish schools inspired by Fethullah Gülen. She is based in Istanbul and wrote about the schools in Pakistan. So how did the Pakistan reporter contribute? How did they cooperate?

This was a story about how the Turkish schools movement was actually quite moderate even though in Turkey it was a big controversial issue. But when you look at these schools they are actually quite moderate and they are nothing like necessarily the more religious schools, hard line schools you might find in much of Pakistan. First of all she is writing about a line of schools which are relevant in Turkey, and have been an issue in Turkey. When you are a correspondent you can travel all over the world. You don't have to just stay in your area. While she is reporting the story, the course of her reporting leads her to Pakistan to illustrate a point about Turkey then it is just simple. First of all it is logical to do that. Secondly, she can tell the correspondents in Pakistan "do you mind if I come and work on this topic as it relates to Turkey?"

Turks and Armenians should try to understand each other

Interview with Pamela Steiner, the great-grand-daughter of Ambassador Morgenthau

H enry Morgenthau was the US ambassador to the Ottoman Empire in 1915, the most troublesome year with the Armenians.

He witnessed how the Turks, desperately hoping to stop further losses, and even regain some of their territory and prior prestige, finally succumbed to German influence and were dragged to collapse.

He was a German Jew, who arrived in New York as an immigrant when he was 10. He was successful in the new country, and through his eventual rise in prominence, he gained President Woodrow Wilson's trust and respect. This ability to gain the confidence of others was characteristic of Ambassador Morgenthau, and greatly contributed to his experience as an ambassador in Turkey.

Despite his ties with Turkish leaders, his experiences recorded first in his diary and then in his book, *Ambassador Morgenthau's Story*, regarding the political environment and the tense situation with the Armenians, led him to change his opinion of his Young Turk associates.

The ambassador's book became a key source for those who acknowledge an Armenian "genocide," as it indicated that the government, hiding behind World War I, had planned and carried out an elimination of the Armenian minority. Ambassador Morgenthau's book was published in Turkish for the first time in 2005 by Belge Publishing Co. Turkish readers can now judge his words for themselves.

Many things have been written about the book from different points of view. Professor H. Lowry in his book *The Story Behind Ambassador Morgenthau's Story* (1990), stated that some of the explanations and arguments in the ambassador's book were inconsistent with the official reports and telegrams that the ambassador sent to the US secretary of state, and inconsistent with entries in the diary that he wrote during the 26 months he spent in Turkey. Lowry also claimed that US journalist Burton J. Hendrick wrote the book.

Approximately half of Ambassador Morgenthau's book focuses on the relationships the ambassador developed during his time in Istanbul. This includes his record of how the Ittihat Terakki (Union and Progress) government became engaged with that of the Germans as, at that time, each believed that their own imperialist aims would be supported by joining forces with the other. The other half of the book contains details of events around the time of the Armenian controversy that Ambassador Morgenthau personally witnessed or that were reported to him from his consuls, Christian missionaries and others in different parts of Turkey.

We talked with Dr. Pamela Steiner, great grandchild of Ambassador Morgenthau, about the memoirs and her approach regarding the current Turkish/Armenian relationship, at the Harvard Humanitarian Initiative of Harvard University, where she is a senior fellow.

Can you please tell us about your family roots?

My mother's parents were Maurice Wertheim and Alma Morgenthau. Alma was one of Ambassador Morgenthau's three daughters and the sister of Henry Morgenthau, Jr., who became Secretary of the Treasury under President Franklin Roosevelt. Alma's (first) husband, Maurice Wertheim, was a banker, art collector, chess player, sportsman and remarkable philanthropist. Alma and Maurice had three daughters. The eldest, Josephine, was my mother. She worked to ban the testing of nuclear weapons and halt the proliferation of nuclear weapons. My father, Ralph Pomerance, a second generation Polish/Lithuanian Jew, was a fine architect.

Can you tell us about yourself? What do you do at Harvard?

As a senior fellow at the Harvard Humanitarian Initiative, I direct the fledging project, "Inter-Communal Violence and Reconciliation." Primarily my work aims to contribute to improving the relationship between the Turkish and Armenian societies. My background includes prior work on the relationships between Germans and Jews, and Israelis and Palestinians. I have a psychotherapy practice, which is private, not connected to Harvard—I specialize in seeing people with psychological trauma.

How are you carrying out this work with Turks and Armenians?

My colleagues and I—people rarely do this work alone—invite individuals who are influential members of both Turkish and Armenian civil societies to participate in confidential dialogue workshops. We structure the workshops to enable participants to learn about each other's perspectives and hear about each other's experiences regarding the relationship of the two communities. After the workshops are over, participants may talk publicly about what they learned, but they have agreed not to reveal the identities of the other participants even then. But, sometimes, at the end of a workshop, participants decide to collaborate on a joint statement or some other project.

Facilitators for these dialogue workshops, such as myself, do not state historical facts or offer opinions about facts. The job of facilitators is to enable participants to talk productively about their communities' history of hurts and losses and their communities' basic needs, fears, concerns and hopes in relation to the community with which they are in conflict. The next step in the workshop is for participants to see if they can contrive a solution that addresses the basic needs, fears, concerns and hopes of both communities.

The participants, not the facilitators, do state the facts, and the characterizations and meaning of those facts, as they know and understand them. I have an educated lay person's opinion about the issues in the Turkish/Armenian relationship, but it is unimportant in this context. What does matter very much is that, while facilitating, I am even-handed and am perceived by participants to be so.

I am well aware, of course, that the use of "genocide" in the context of the Armenian/Turkish relationship has an enormous but different meaning to each community and different meanings to different sub-groups within each community. I might ask participants in a workshop to discuss the importance of these different meanings with each other.

But your great-grand father did not use the term "genocide" in his book, right?

Yes, that's true. The word "genocide" did not exist when my great grandfather wrote his book. He wrote some now famous descriptions of what he witnessed and learned. Here are two examples from his book that we are discussing, *Ambassador Morgenthau's Story*:

"Talaat's attitude toward the Armenians was summed up in the proud boast which he made to his friends: 'I have accomplished more toward solving the Armenian problem in three months than Abdul Hamid accomplished in thirty years!'" (p. 234)

"From him (Dr. Lepsius, a German missionary) Enver scarcely concealed the official purpose. Dr. Lepsius was simply staggered by his frankness, for Enver told him in so many words that they at last had an opportunity to rid themselves of the Armenians and that they proposed to use it." (p. 235).

What is your impression about the book generally?

It's such an extraordinary close-up history about a fascinating period. It's the sum of the many aspects of the book that I find so remarkable. He knew everybody and was an acute observer. There's a tremendous amount of detail about his relations with the diplomatic community and the Young Turks. He did not go to Istanbul aiming to do something in particular for the Turks or Armenians over and above what an ambassador does. He did not arrive with a personal interest in the Armenians. He got along very well with the Turks and talks about what he admired in them. He stresses how sincere the Young Turks were initially in their aim to put Turkey on a democratic path. He notes how they failed at this and how this failure partly led these leaders to revert to what he characterized as much more "primitive" governance.

As one of the top people, he bore witness to the fate of the Armenians, and protested about it widely. It was also emotionally painful for both him and his wife to witness. He records his efforts to stop the killings of Armenians and how his failure led him to leave Istanbul.

Yet, at the same time, he conveyed a deep understanding of the Turks' struggles. He understood how the Turkish leaders felt humiliated by their losses of territory. He saw and was horrified by the suffering of ordinary Turks during this period, as a result of their leaders' attempts to regain by going to war that lost territory and prestige. He reported in detail all he learned about how the Germans manipulated and drew the Turks into the war. However, I understand that contemporary historians consider that he overrated the influence of the Germans, though I believe that most agree that German influence was great.

So why then does nobody mention the responsibility Germany bears for the incidents that took place in 1915?

This is a very important question, as is the question of responsibility more generally, though the word would need to be defined first. It would be interesting to discuss this question with historians, which of course I am not, but also with psychologists, which I am. But it isn't true that no one mentions German responsibility, if "responsibility" is understood as Germany's exercising influence on and acting in complicity with the commitment of certain acts. For example, Taner Akcam's *A Shameful Act* and Donald Bloxham's *The Great Game of Genocide* both discuss Germany's role. And one of my great grandfather's book's chapters is actually entitled "Germany Forces Turkey into War." Whatever German responsibility was, though, does not ease the responsibilities of the Ittihat ve Terakki Party.

It has been claimed that the book was not written by your great grand-grandfather, but by Burton J. Hendrick, the famous journalist of the time. What do you know about this claim?

I don't know that. But I know that Hendrick stayed at my grandfather's house and they worked together on the book. My grandfather had a diary. In the book he mentions when he is quoting from the diary. My grandfather was not a trained writer. So it is very natural to get some professional support, a ghostwriter. But you very easily notice his "voice" while reading the book.

Is Armenian identity constructed on hostility towards Turks? Is this something healthy?

Some Armenians feel hostile to Turks as a whole. Some Armenians feel hostile not only to the Turks of that time, but also to Turks today who do not know and do not acknowledge what the Turks did to the Armenians in those years. But not all Armenians today feel the same about all Turks, although for perhaps all Armenians the memories of the past are very painful. Their pain increases when people minimize those hurts.

So what do you think should be done?

I think 1915-23 were particularly terrible years and there has been an important gap between the two sets of communities since then. My understanding is that most members of these two sets of communities don't now know each other. They need to know each other. What happened in 1915-1923 should be discussed today, and they all should gain greater understanding of each other.

What else?

We have already been talking about conflict resolution and reconciliation processes. One element in the process is the creation of public knowledge of what happened. The past must be dealt with. This includes, of course, the historical facts and the different narratives incorporating those facts, the different meanings of those facts to the different communities. There must be greater such knowledge and understanding of each other.

A second element is public acknowledgment of those facts and perspectives. Not only do both communities need to tell what happened, and how they understand it; but each party must acknowledge the other's narrative—assuming they believe that the other is being sincere. Such a process can lead to deep understanding and empathy, and eventually to solutions.

I believe that the achievement of these two elements, truth and acknowledgment, would make an enormous, positive difference in the Armenian-Turkish relationship.

The only way to combat bias is to be more proactive

Interview with Nida Khan, Muslim-American journalist

N ida Khan says Muslims in the US and throughout the world are cognizant of the bias towards them in the media as they're often caricatured as the "other" or something "foreign," resulting in an inaccurate portrayal of a diverse group.

Khan is an independent journalist and producer working in both print and radio. She is currently a news correspondent with WRKS 98.7 KISS FM NY and is a member of the production team for the station's broadcasts "Open Line" and "The Week in Review." In addition to her work at KISS FM, she is the fill-in executive producer on Rev. Al Sharpton's nationally syndicated show "Keeping it Real."

Khan shares her insight about the world of media and talks about the unfortunate bias about Muslims/Islam in the media. As a Muslim-American journalist, she stresses we need more producers, executives and people behind the scenes who can call on experts/individuals they know, who can provide a more balanced, fair, and accurate depiction of an issue.

Khan previously served as editor-in-chief of *elan*: The Guide to Global Muslim Culture and has contributed pieces for such diverse outlets as *The Associated Press, New York Daily News, The Source, AOL BVX, The Huffington Post, XXL, The Grio* and more. She focuses on Muslim discrimination issues in the US. I interviewed Khan on her personal experience in American media as a Muslim-American journalist.

Can you please tell us about yourself?

I've been a writer since I was literally 8 or 9 years old, writing poetry, etc. I always had two passions in life: music and news. Because I was always fascinated with news, politics, media and, of course, writing, I decided to major in journalism when I was in college, but I interned and worked at record labels and different places within the music industry. Even after graduating from school, I continued to work in the music biz and slowly began writing for various entertainment publications.

After working for different music magazines and freelancing with the entertainment division at *The Associated Press*, I slowly began moving towards news and politics for the simple reason that I needed something a little more substantive in life. Bottom line, interviewing famous musicians, writing about flashy cars (yes, I did that too!) and attending parties can be fun, but I could not see myself doing that for the rest of my life. And with so much madness going on in the world, I felt it was my duty to write, cover, and discuss real issues that have a real life impact in people's lives (as corny as that may sound). I was always keenly politically aware, but the final push that moved me into news/politics was when I lost my own father in a horrific tragedy in 2005 that involved bias, police misconduct, etc. From that point on, it's been more in-depth issues, and I haven't looked back since.

Would you be willing to tell us about your father's death?

It was on March 6, 2005, when my father, a devoted husband and parent of four, was leaving a grocery store in a small, conservative neighborhood in New Jersey. This was a routine trip for the architect who first came to the United States nearly four decades prior.

As he exited this grocery store, an SUV failed to yield to the pedestrian and struck him. He flew back several feet, landed on his back, sustained massive head trauma and virtually lost his ability to speak. In '05, at the height of Bush-era hostility and an "us vs. them" mentality, the police and paramedics of this town arrived at the scene and without properly assessing the extent of my father's injuries, automatically assumed that he could not speak English.

They noted "language barrier" on their report and sent him to a non-trauma hospital (despite the fact that there was a trauma facility equally close by). It wasn't until nearly five hours later that he was transferred to a trauma hospital, by which time my father had fallen into a deep coma. He died three days later.

Tell us a little bit about the stories you cover.

In terms of telling stories, there have been so many moving and fascinating people and ideas I've had the opportunity to write and report about. Interviewing Malcolm X's daughter was one of the highlights, as was interviewing a Pakistani woman and daughter whose husband/father was murdered following the 9/11 attacks. Covering instances of police brutality, like the case of Sean Bell here in New York, and attending countless protests/rallies across the nation always stays with me. It's been a broad range of stories, but the most meaningful ones, like a Palestinian midwife who saved the lives of hundreds of women in the Gaza Strip, are the ones that motivate me to continue doing the work that I'm doing.

Do you think there is a bias about Islam or Muslims in American media?

There is without a doubt an unfortunate bias about Muslims/Islam in the media. Sadly, virtually the only time Muslims are mentioned in the press is in the context of a terrorist attack, or some other form of terror. They're often caricatured as the "other" or something "foreign," and the result is a blatantly inaccurate portrayal of perhaps the most diverse body of people. And even when issues involving Islam, Arabs or the "Muslim world" come up, many networks/publications will go to an "expert" that is neither Muslim nor Arab. Muslims in the US (and beyond) are, of course, cognizant of this bias. Not only do we need more journalists who can tell our stories, we need more producers, executives and people behind the scenes that can call on experts/individuals they know, who can provide a more balanced, fair and accurate depiction of an issue. Diversity in news doesn't simply mean faces of color sitting at an anchor desk, but real diversity in the newsroom. Since people bring their life experiences wherever they go, you need a multitude of voices in any newsroom if you plan on delivering the truth.

As a Muslim reporter in New York have you ever felt discriminated against?

All of this is easier said than done, of course. I myself have faced certain institutional blockades; in fact, that's why I chose to freelance full-time a little over four years ago. Unable to obtain employment in '06, despite having extensive experience, I decided to freelance in both print and radio, and thankfully it has panned out and even afforded me greater opportunities than I would have ever received stuck full-time in God knows what position at just one news organization.

Tell us about your Huffington Post experience. Many journalists cringe at the Huffington Post business model (one in which most contributors are not paid for their work). Where does the "HuffPo" model fit into the future of journalism?

Huffington Post—where I do contribute pieces from time to time—does in fact receive criticism from people (especially more so now that they have merged with AOL). Although people (including myself) would love to see more funds, HuffPo did create the perfect model for news in this day and age, and going forward. Even though they don't pay their bloggers much, if anything, they also don't charge a fee for their content. That being said, I feel people should be compensated for their work, so hopefully things will change in the future. Who knows? For now, HuffPo offers increased exposure and an avenue for people to voice their ideas who may otherwise be limited to doing so in the mainstream press.

Given what has happened to newspapers in the last few years, what skills do you recommend that new journalists should further develop?

New journalists should try to master everything. If you don't know how to shoot and edit video, learn it. If you've never worked equipment in a studio, master it. If you want to better understand the digital world, start today. With more and more newspapers, networks and other media outlets eliminating full-time jobs every day, the more multifaceted you are the better. Nowadays, being a jack-of-all-trades is a tremendous advantage. Learn as many facets of media as you can, especially since everything is converging into one entity online. I'm working on mastering more myself.

Is the blogosphere an adequate substitute for journalism? What blogs do you subscribe to?

The blogosphere is an interesting place. On the one hand it's a great avenue for issues to be addressed that are often ignored by the mainstream press. On the other, many bloggers have not endured the rigorous process of being properly trained as journalists. Often times, there isn't enough fact checking and research being done by bloggers, and that truly affects the integrity and credibility of your piece. And because blogs try to churn out as much original content as possible, even editors may not take the appropriate time to thoroughly check a piece. It's clearly not a perfect journalism model, but it is the way of the future, so it's just a matter of working out these kinks.

I subscribe to a bunch of blogs, I pretty much try to read everything—progressive, mainstream and conservative.

How do you think social media has affected the recent developments in the Middle East? Is that effect overstated?

Social media obviously played a massive role in the recent Mideast uprisings, especially in places like Egypt. The April 6th Movement, in fact, started as a Facebook movement—if I'm not mistaken—and a lot of the organizing was facilitated online. Because it was a youth uprising, young folks used the mechanisms they were most comfortable with and accustomed to. Even reporters here in the States (myself included) were getting much of our information from Twitter, thanks to people on the ground who were tweeting developments. Even major networks like CNN and MSNBC were citing people's tweets (of course stating that they couldn't independently verify the info). But just from that perspective alone, you cannot diminish the very real impact social media had in Egypt and elsewhere.

Are all newspapers folding? Or is it just some? Which ones and why them?

Not all newspapers are folding, of course, but many are getting rid of their international bureaus and full-time reporting positions. They are relying more and more heavily on freelancers, which isn't necessarily a bad thing in terms of having a variety of voices, but it isn't fair to journalists seeking stability in an already chaotic business. As far as bureaus shutting down, however, that's another story. If you do not have people on the ground, then you cannot properly report on issues or tell the story. And this leads to an unfortunate separation of the US from the rest of the world at a time when we are becoming more globalized than ever.

Many people do love the feel of something tangible in their hands, but at the same time, many young people have never even picked up an actual newspaper in their lives. It may seem strange, but it is a reality in the digital age where everything is virtually available with the click of a button. And because of this disconnect between the old and young, papers are struggling to maintain their revenue, and thus shutting down.

If newspapers are struggling to generate print advertising revenue, will they have any more luck generating online ad revenue?

The notion of online revenue is very interesting. Plenty of sites generate a great deal of revenue from advertising and are thus able to offer content for free to users. But even that idea is being tested. Papers like *The New York Times* are now charging a fee for folks to read their news online. It will be interesting to see if users will remain devoted in the long run. Guess we will all just have to wait and see.

I believe that the Holy God speaks to us in the Qur'an

Interview with Professor Walter Wagner,
Moravian College and Theological Seminary

After carefully reading the Qur'an and examining it based on his many years of study, a leading American theologian has concluded that via the holy book God is speaking to all human beings around the world, a voice that, in his astonishing book, he said he tried to transmit to readers and students, as well to himself, to deepen his understanding.

Opening the Qur'an is definitely a bewildering and inspiring book, not only for the non-Muslim and English-speaking readers, but also Muslim readers. Wagner "opens" the Qur'an by offering a comprehensive and extraordinarily readable, step-by-step introduction to the text, making it accessible to everyone who is interested in Islam and Islam's holy book.

Wagner is an adjunct professor of theology at Moravian College and Theological Seminary. He is the author of a number of books, including *After the Apostles: Christianity in the Second Century*.

Wagner tells us in this interview of his extraordinary journey to the Qur'an and its message and speaks in detail about the impressive book he says he wrote for himself. However, what he particularly explains during the interview are the similarities in the way that God approached people in different holy books and how Prophets are described in them. He says: "I think what we share is that there is one God who calls us to be obedient to this one God—that this God calls us to create a community of faithful people who are dedicated to doing the will of this one God, the worship of this one God. There is more in common along these lines."

*At first your work focused on early Christianity, particularly
the time of the Apostles, so how did you get inspired to write a
book about the Qur'an?*

The book has come out of my own teaching for a little more than 20
years. I think I am just beginning to understand the Qur'an. But actually,
because of the relationships between Judaism, Christianity, and Islam,
we come together, not only in some areas about theology and our culture, but also we come together in terms of our histories.

There have been times in which we have bumped heads and other
times in which we have clashed with weapons. But we have also come to
worship the same God. And in doing that, there should be, out of my own
teaching experience, a way to try to understand another religion, which
takes effort. For a teacher it takes effort [to teach], but the one who
learns the most is the teacher.

So the book has come out of my own teaching experience and I have
been very fortunate to have experiences with Muslim men and women
as well, particularly with the Turkish community in the last seven years.
One of the driving forces of the book was to explain all of this to myself
and then to others, particularly in this important time where we must
understand each other.

So, can it be said that you actually wrote this book for yourself?

Yes. You will find that authors have voices. Those of you who are Muslim
may know who is speaking in the Qur'an. But who is speaking in this
[Wagner's] book? Sometimes it's an academic voice; the professor speaks.
Sometimes it's a personal voice. The use of even the "you" pronoun, where
I have to make decisions about what I think, and sometimes it will also be
a "we" voice. What can "we" say together and what are the differences and
what can the resemblances be? So yes, I try to speak in those voices.

*What was the "voice" that came to mind when you were
reading the Qur'an? Who was speaking?*

I believe the Qur'an is an inspired book. I believe that God has inspired
many persons and many Prophets and messengers and within the Qur'an
it is the voice of the Holy God who speaks to us—the voice of justice and
peace, the voice of speaking about human beings who need to live
together in peace and also to work together for the rest of the world. So

yes, that was a voice, which I heard, and a voice, which I then tried to transmit to readers and students, as well to myself, to deepen my understanding.

I'm not sure whether you can read Arabic, but it is likely you focused on translations. Could you tell us about your methodology? How did you work? How did you study?

Perhaps as a non-Muslim, reading the Qur'an for the first couple of times is a bewildering experience. For those of us who come from a biblical tradition the expectation is that it is going to read like Genesis, Exodus or the Gospel of Mark; it's going to have a storyline. Yet you have pieces that are in sections, which are knitted together into a whole. It takes several readings, ponderings and plenty of head scratching to understand. But I guess the first step is to not be discouraged. The first suggestion is to read it from the back to the front, to try and understand the Prophet, peace be upon him. It also takes reading not only the Qur'an but also what others have said.

What similarities and differences have you found between the biblical tradition and the Qur'an?

I think the fundamental difference, without going into the 30 biblical characters which are shared, would be the issue of the nature of the Bible and the nature of the Qur'an. One of the things I think, and Muslim students I have had would testify to this, would be that we are operating sometimes with the same language and the same words, but we are also operating with different principles, with different assumptions and we need to clarify those assumptions.

For Muslims the Qur'an, every word, every letter where things are placed, are all given by God. That is not the case for Christians and the Bible. Christians do not give special attention or reverence to one particular language. We are comfortable with translations. I am comfortable with manuscript variations, with different accounts of the same story, while Muslim students may come and say "what is it really?" As a Christian I am not bothered by different versions. But as a teacher I must be careful to explain this to my Muslim students and learn from them about their approach in turn and explain this to a non-Muslim audience.

We share so many Prophets yet our expectations of them are different. We can gain from difference, though, by trying to understand what the "intention of the account" is. I think what we share is [the belief] that there is one God who calls us to be obedient to this one God—that this God calls us to create a community of faithful people who are dedicated to doing the will of this one God, the worship of this one God. There is more in common along these lines. Perhaps a major difference, though, is along the lines of what a messenger is, what a Prophet is. In Islam among the things a Prophet would be, first not only would they be inspired, but also to be perfect. It seems from my experiences with my Muslim students, when they read the Bible, they would say about David committing adultery and murdering, for example, that this would be reprehensible to a Muslim. To them the question would be "how could you follow someone who is such a sinner?"

Can you please tell us about how Jesus, Prophet Muhammad and others are portrayed in the holy books of Christianity and Islam? What are some similarities and differences?

My Muslim students always surprise their Christian classmates by saying that in order to be a good Muslim "you have to believe in Jesus." Jesus was born of a virgin. He performs miracles, he feeds, he heals, he raises the dead, and he is called Messiah and will come again at the end of the age to be part of the judgment. He was a teacher; he had disciples and called on people to follow the way of God. So these are some of the similarities of the portrayal of Jesus in the Qur'an. You will notice that I left out crucifixion and resurrection because those are the key differences [between Christianity and Islam].

In regards to some of the others, like Moses for example, the Qur'an speaks about traditions that Jews have had. Part of what you have in the Qur'an you would find in early Jewish writings, so when the Qur'an speaks of these things, there is a connection. I would say not a contradiction, but a connection. And as I understand it in my simple way, Moses came and set up governmental structure and Jesus is the one who came and gave a spiritual meaning [to people] without any political agenda. Christians would later add that component. But Prophet Muhammad comes and he is the one for Islam who has both the "earthly side," you could say, and the spiritual side and brings them together. Both of these Prophets are coming from the same tradition of a God, who loves and cares for the world, so must you.

How have you been impacted by your study of the Qur'an? Has it changed your life in anyway?

I think that amongst one of the very important ways that it did is that I have come to understand Islam and the Qur'an in terms of prayer; there is a profound sense of the holiness of prayer and that a life can be framed by prayer. My little understanding of Islam has led me to recognize that it is a religion that is grounded in the theology of creation. This to me has tremendous ethical ramifications and when I look at others I recognize that they too are God's representatives to care of the world.

Can you please talk a little bit about the structure and narrative of the Qur'an?

Well, I attempt in the book to deal with the structure and I use the idea of "the straight way." I see what God has given, and in the Qur'an and also in the Old and New Testaments, he has given a pathway, a pathway from the beginning of the world or of a person's life to "the destination." For example, in the construction of a road, when you go out there and see the workers digging in the road, they just don't start putting the asphalt right on top of the dirt. You have to have a proper foundation. And I think that foundation is what the Qur'an is, yes, it is the road, the science of the Qur'an. You have to have a foundation and that means you have to go deeper into the Qur'an than what seems to be on the surface.

If you just take the Qur'an or the Book of Leviticus or some other sacred literature on the surface, you might be able to answer one of my pop quizzes. You need to see that there is depth, and that the depth is a spiritual depth about the entirety of God's plan for the world. It's God who laid out the road. Once you understand it as the outline and as the essence, you then begin to understand the structure of who is being addressed in this set of stories. Where are the transitions? What is the reasoning behind it? What does this point to? It will point to the one God, to the structure of a life, a community and individuals. Then you will understand why there are divorce issues, why there are family law issues. This is the stuff of regular life. How do you find God in the midst of your daily life? And then as you progress, who are the persons who can inspire, and who are the persons and the tendencies that you should avoid?

We know there is criticism in Western circles about the way that women are portrayed in Muslim societies. So could you tell us about how women are portrayed in the Qur'an?

First, I think it is important to understand that men and women are equal before God. Men and women are responsible for their own ultimate destinies. A woman can find her way to the hellfire just as easily as a man. A woman can find her way into heaven as easily as a man. There is a profound theological, religious equality. There are social distinctions in the Qur'an and the West doesn't like to hear that. The distinctions [between men and women] are that there are some physical aspects in terms of muscle power and responsibility. I can remember accidentally being part of a marriage counseling session when I was going to see an imam in upper Manhattan. I thought I had an appointment with him, and they told me to sit down while he was talking to a brother and sister who were trying to get her husband to do the right thing. The imam was very clear. He simply said the Qur'an says it's the husband's responsibility to make sure that the family is supported. There should be no deadbeat dads in Islam. It is the wife's responsibility to help raise and build up the family. If there are going to be any jobs outside—that you will negotiate. There is a negotiation of equality in a marriage contract.

And then who takes care of widows? It should be the sons. I think in the West this is not usually seen; there's an assumption that a widow will have to be on her own and take care of herself. There is much more of a sense of community in the Qur'an. When a marriage takes place and there's difficulty between husband and wife, it can be settled when you bring in the family. You are joining people together in a community. There ought to be a community built on compassion, love, and justice. I think the Qur'an speaks to that. What happens culturally—that cultural bubble that we live in—can be so influential and sometimes it's justified by some religious text pulled out of context. We can do that as easily as not.

I think there is another stereotype concerning Islam and verses about jihad in the Qur'an. So how do you think we should interpret the verses about jihad?

There are different interpretations in Islam. It becomes an issue of historical context. For example, when was the "sword" *ayah* [verse] revealed, and under what context, and how do you deal with that? Does the sword *ayah* aggregate all the other *ayahs*? I think it's important if you know the root for "jihad" simply means "exertion" or "struggle." I say it to my students: "It's jihad. You have to reason and use your head." Sometimes students are less willing to struggle to use their knowledge. But out of the 35 or 36 mentions in the Qur'an of the root for jihad, only about five deal with the military. What you have is vital struggle for God. The Qur'an obviously is not a "turn the other cheek" book. It comes out of struggle and war, out of the struggle the community had in order to survive.

In the Qur'an and in Islamic tradition, there is no mistreatment of prisoners. No mistreatment of noncombatants. You don't use napalm against people who have pistols. You do not mistreat the environment. You don't do what Saddam Hussein did upon his withdrawal from Kuwait in 1991 and burn the oil fields. You don't destroy. You fight only until the enemy surrenders or you have an armistice.

When we look at countries in the Middle East and North Africa that were colonized by Western countries, do you think the justification for the misinterpretation of these verses is due to colonization? Was it a reaction to the West?

Yes, I think that's an accurate description. I think you are kind in your description, in that the Western (you can throw in the Soviet Union) justification was that we have the right way and we're going to impose this way because we know what truth is. I always get suspicious of people—my academic field is heresy—because you always find that when you take a legitimate position and drive it to an extreme, that's dangerous. And if you have injustice being done, sometimes it is justified by a cross or by a Marxist approach or whatever it might be. That is a distortion of the religion, whether it's the crescent and the star or the cross. I think that what we don't know is the history of what can be called the Middle East, whatever that might be. We romanticize the Crusades in the West; we turn Crusaders into comic book characters. We have no understanding of the real politics and the relationships.

Tell me about the feedback you have received so far on the book. Has there been criticism from the Muslim community or Christian circles?

I can answer that more easily about the Christian circles. By and large, those people who are looking for peace and understanding like the book.

Those people who believe that only they have the truth and the truth is one way and everybody else is damned include me amongst the damned. They have been vocal to say that in some minor circles. There are those who think, and this holds for anybody that gets involved in interreligious dialogue, that there is risk involved.

I think I use an anecdote at the beginning of the book, I was teaching a class on "Introduction to Islam" to college students and I had a Pakistani student who was furious with me. He felt that since I was saying positive things about the Qur'an that I must convert and he was appalled that I wouldn't. In the same class, I had a young lady come up to me and say, "when are you going to expose Islam as the work of the devil?" And so there you are in between the two, but then you have others who come and say to you that this has been a good adventure. I am now learning about others. But I have found on the part of Muslims, and maybe it's just the ones who speak to me, but I have found that they say, "thank God you are speaking about this." I believe that there needs to be what I call "hinge people," people who can swing between the two sides and maintain their own integrity.